AF251504

CINCINNATI, OHIO

ISBN: 0-944094-44-9

Published by:
ST Books
ST Media Group International Inc.
407 Gilbert Avenue
Cincinnati, Ohio 45202
Tel. 513-421-2050
Fax 513-421-6110
E-mail: books@stmediagroup.com
www.stmediagroup.com/stbooks

Distributed to the U.S. book and art trade by:
Watson-Guptill Publications
770 Broadway
New York, NY 10003
www.watsonguptill.com

Distributed outside the U.S. to the book and art trade by:
Harper Design International
HarperCollins International
10 East 53rd Street
New York, NY 10022
www.harpercollins.com/hdi

Book design by Kim Pegram, Art Director, VM+SD
Book edited by Alicia Hanson, Associate Editor, VM+SD

Printed in China
10 9 8 7 6 5 4 3 2 1

# With Liberty and Retail for All

# E∗Trading Retail Spaces

# Independents Day

WITH LIBERTY AND RETAIL FOR ALL

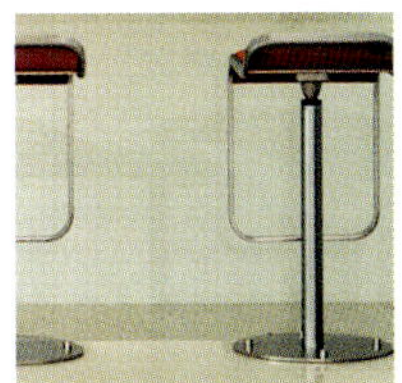

# 5

# STORES AND RETAIL SPACES

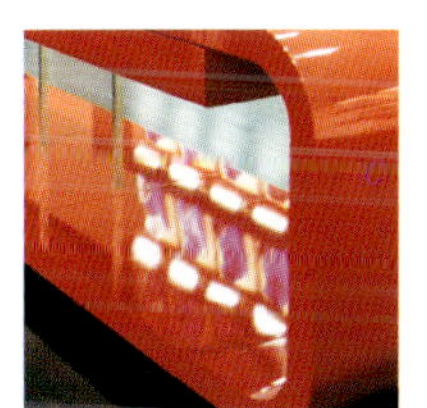

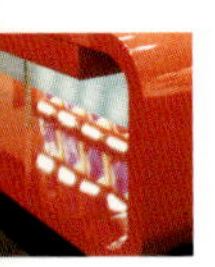

# Liberty

Regent Street, London

*20/20 Ltd., London*

Liberty's Regent Street department store is one of the grande dames of London retailing, with origins dating back to 1875. But in recent years, the once-powerful British department store brand had begun to lose some of its luster. So, the retailer hired 20/20 Ltd. (London) to help revitalize the Liberty brand by redesigning its three-floor, 40,000-square-foot space on Regent Street. (Liberty's adjoining Tudor House retail space is also slated to be updated within the next few years.)

Simon Stacey, 20/20's creative partner, says this was more than a facelift or modernization. The Regent Street project "involved a precise definition of what Liberty represents, and using this insight to remain faithful to the brand when creating the new store design." That effort resulted in the creation of an "aesthetic emporium" that reflects the design-centered ethos of the store's founder, Arthur Lasenby Liberty, who began his business by selling silks, embroideries, furniture, carpeting and curios imported from Japan, China, Java and Persia.

To help pay tribute to the Liberty store's long history, 20/20 designers created a new, Edwardian-style entrance at the corner of Regent and Great Marlborough streets. Hanging in the entrance's porch/reception area is a light sculpture that pulses with varying intensities of light, to give the space a sense of movement.

Inside, the store's escalator has been moved to the front, giving customers using the new entrance easy access to either the women's shoes and lingerie departments on the second floor or to the menswear department in the lower level. The ground floor also features contemporary chandeliers and oak "play tables" displaying cosmetics and other beauty-related merchandise.

Visitors to the second story encounter a series of raised "shoe stages," which encourage customers to pick up the footwear. The lower level is home to a new café/restaurant called Arthur's, and the adjoining menswear displays include a 100-foot-long shirt wall and red-lacquer fixtures holding neckties that harken back to the mod 1960s.

"There is a richness and color in the Liberty brand heritage," says Liberty managing director John Ball, "which we think is reflected in the new store design."

**CLIENT**
Liberty, London – John Ball, managing director; Phil Looker, store planner; Barbara King, visual merchandising and product

**DESIGN**
20/20 Ltd., London – Rune Gustafson, managing director; Bernard Dooling, board director; Simon Stacey, creative partner; Jeff MacCall, client partner; Sarah Chapman, Sarah Hilden, Andrea Vaughan, designers

**GENERAL CONTRACTORS**
A.E. Hadley, Portsmouth, U.K.; John Richards Shopfitters, Saltash, U.K.

**ARCHITECT**
Landmark Architecture Ltd., London

**OUTSIDE DESIGN CONSULTANTS**
Into Lighting, London; Neil Wilkins, Wiltshire, U.K.

**SUPPLIERS**
Chorus, London (audio/video, ceiling, flooring); A.E. Handley, Portsmouth, U.K. (fixturing, furniture); 20/20 Ltd., London (graphics, signage, wallcoverings); Neil Wilkins, Wiltshire, U.K. (light sculpture)

**PHOTOGRAPHY**
Adrian Wilson, Macclesfield, U.K.

DRIES VAN NOTEN

prettypretty
Cosmetics
& Fragrance

# El Palacio de Hierra

Puebla, Mexico

*Pavlik Design Team, Fort Lauderdale, Fla.*

The large Mexico City-based fashion retailer was expanding outside its home city for the first time ever, and wanted to establish itself as the ultimate upscale fashion and home destination in the newly developing Puebla retail market.

The themes that Pavlik Design Team (Fort Lauderdale, Fla.) brought to the project were "bold" and "contemporary."

In creating a structure visible from the adjacent highway, a stainless-steel paneled façade and entrance doors were inspired by local Colonial architecture.

The two-level, 300,000-square-foot store features an open plan, to visually enlarge the space with distinctive fashion worlds radiating from a soaring glass-domed atrium. Wide fashion boulevards connect plazas and streets of shops. High, luminous ceilings with kinetic light coves define circulation and pull traffic through the bright, airy spaces.

**CLIENT**
El Palacio de Hierra, Mexico City – Jose Maria Blanco, general director; George Aguirre, sub-director, construction & remodels; Mauricio Camacho, project manager

**DESIGN**
Pavlik Design Team, Fort Lauderdale, Fla. – R.J. Pavlik, president/ceo; Luis Valladares, director, design; Luis Martin, vp; Patricia Dominguez, project designer; Manuel Cordero, Diana Santiago, project managers; Javier Calle, planner; Amy Ann Straley, lighting designer

**ARCHITECT**
Sordo Madaleno Architectos, Mexico City

**SUPPLIERS**
Eykon Wallsource, Memphis, Tenn., Innovations, New York, Maharam, Hollywood, Fla., Maya Romanoff, Chicago (wallcoverings/fabrics); Atlas, Los Angeles, Bentley, City of Industry, Calif., Iberia Tiles, Hauppauge, N.Y., Innovative Marble & Tile, Hauppauge, N.Y. (flooring); Formica, Lithia Springs, Ga., Lamin-Art, Elk Grove Village, Ill., Wilsonart, Miami (laminates); Knoll Textiles, Miami, Lightblocks, Amherst, N.H., Southwest Progressive, Richardson, Texas (special finishes)

**PHOTOGRAPHY**
Myro Rosky, Fort Lauderdale, Fla.

ADOLFO DOMINGUEZ
NAUTICA

TICA
NAUTICA

# Ports 1961 at Ogilvy's

Montreal

*Aedifica Inc., Montreal*

Ports Intl. is one of the largest specialty retailers in China, with a fleet of 200 stores. But it began life 41 years ago in Toronto, and wanted to re-establish itself in its homeland.

Determined to reintegrate the North American marketplace, it hired Aedifica Inc. (Montreal) to design a new shop prototype that would break away from its conservative past. The Ogilvy shop represents the first of three Canadian applications.

The design challenges were: to make a fashion statement; to connect with a younger high-end audience, one that values simplicity and modernity; to stand for high-quality materials and detailing; to create a simple backdrop for the high-end merchandise; to leverage Ports' past by using materials traditionally specified for Ports; and to convey a great sense of space despite limited square footage.

Walnut and marble, Ports' traditional materials, were reinterpreted into a modern aesthetic. A thematic glass/wood back wall (which designers called "the forest") anchors the cashwrap. The cashwrap itself was wrapped in glass so it could showcase smaller products.

Recessed tracks running the full length of the walls allowed discreet fixturing while maximizing the merchandising opportunities. Merchandising of smaller items was carried on across "the forest" in a clear glass cage floating off of the floor.

**CLIENT**
Ports 1961, Toronto – Fiona Cibanni, senior vp, design; Brian Anyon, senior vp, development

**DESIGN**
Aedifica Inc., Montreal – Jean-Pierre Genereux, partner-in-charge; Evangeline Guerra, designer; Jean-Luc Touikan, senior designer; Hrant Boghossian, computer graphics

**GENERAL CONTRACTOR**
Anjinnov, Montreal

**SUPPLIERS**
Draperies de l'est, Montreal, Les agences Pierre Breton, Montreal (fabrics); Ebenisterie Pierre Arsenault, Mascouche, Que. (fixturing); Peerless, Montreal, Sistemalux, Montreal (lighting); Mignapro, Montreal (signage)

**PHOTOGRAPHY**
Michel Tremblay, Montreal

# Taste

Vancouver International Airport

*The Buchan Group, Melbourne, Australia*

The Taste store at Vancouver International Airport was the first of a new retail confectionery concept developed by Nuance Group's global franchising division (Sydney, Australia). The format was designed to be adaptable to a variety of environments, from a shop-in-shop to a traditional mid-size store.

The idea was that Taste sell sugar-based confections aimed at an adult market. In this case, it also had to appeal to an adult market that was rushing through an airport, concerned about meeting people and making flights.

A completely open storefront maximizes exposure to the concourse by the use of angled wall space and the total clarity of store fixtures, creating a dynamic and inviting retail offer to capture shoppers on the run as well as those with time to browse.

Wall and merchandising units are finished in high-quality sprayed paint, back-painted glass and accents of brushed stainless steel. Colorful images of the confectionery flavors are used throughout the store. White packaging reinforces the interior concept.

A bulkhead provides security and enables signage to be placed at strategic heights. Wall units are broken by a vertical visual merchandising and tasting station.

**CLIENT**
The Nuance Group, Sydney, Australia – Penny Baker, vp

**DESIGN**
The Buchan Group, Melbourne, Australia – David Roocke, associate director; Rodney Valentine, senior interior designer

**SUPPLIERS**
Pancor, Vancouver (fabrics, fixturing, flooring, furniture, lighting, laminates); Viagraphics, Vancouver (signage and graphics)

**PHOTOGRAPHY**
Martin Tessler, Vancouver

DUTY & TAX FREE CANDY
CONFISERIE HORS TAXES
TASTE
CANADIAN
DUTY & TAX FREE CANDY
CONFISERIE HORS TAXES
TASTE

GIFT BOX
Princess
C$39.25
GIFT BOX
Sweet Success
C$45.25
GIFT BOX
C$49.60

TASTE
DUTY & TAX FREE CANDY
TASTE
CONFISERIE HORS TAXES
DUTY & TAX FREE CANDY
CONFISERIE HORS TAXES
*FREE

## Seattle Seahawks
## Pro Shop

Seahawks Stadium, Seattle

*5ifth Floor, Seattle*

Most professional sports franchises see their retail programs as novelties, and place them on a level other than the mainstay hot dog and beer sales.

A few, though, see the revenue and brand-building opportunities in thousands of fans wearing, waving or wanting their logo merchandise — especially in the televised images accompanying the game.

When computer whiz Paul Allen bought the Seattle Seahawks football team and imploded the ailing Kingdome in favor of a new, modern stadium, he wanted to build a large central retail store within to capitalize on both game-day traffic and downtown foot traffic.

Design firm 5ifth Floor (Seattle) was retained to design a 2900-square-foot store with access from both the stadium's interior concourse and the street adjacent to the stadium. The Seahawks wanted the store to be an icon establishing "the home of the Seahawks" – powerful, modern and sophisticated through its use of graphics, audio/visual equipment and sleek, clean fixtures.

The store is a wide and shallow 100-by-29 feet, and about 90 percent of the walls are floor-to-ceiling windows. So the store had to be able to draw and accommodate a large number of customers and move them quickly and smoothly. Bold, clear signage and displays (by product type) help customers find quickly what they want and make their way to one of eight points of sale. And those sales are 115 percent above projections.

CLIENT
Seattle Seahawks – Tom Chiado, Sue Harris, Lance Lopes

DESIGN
5ifth Floor, Seattle – Eduardo Alfonso, Bryan Berg, Rebecca Jack, Alexandra Ramsden, Scott Truitt

ARCHITECT
DKA Architects, Seattle – Donna Brown

GENERAL CONTRACTOR
Turner Construction, Seattle

OUTSIDE DESIGN CONSULTANT
Candela Architectural Lighting Design, Seattle

SUPPLIERS
Robelan, New York (fixturing); Maverick Specialty Contracting, Seattle (flooring); Super Graphics, Seattle (signage and graphics); Robelan, New York (mannequins and forms)

PHOTOGRAPHY
Steve Keating, Seattle

INSTINCT
DRIVE TO COMPETE
PRO-LINE
PRO-LINE
PRO-LINE

PREY
PURSUIT OF THE
GOAL LINE
CAPS
SEATTLE SEAHAWKS
SEATTLE SEAHAWKS

INSTINCT
SEAHAWKS
PRO·SHOP
SEAHAWKS
SEAHAWKS
SEAHAWKS
SEAHAWKS

# Miss Sixty

South Coast Plaza, Costa Mesa, Calif.

*Borruso & Alessandro Design, Venice, Calif.*

The 3400-square-foot location in South Coast Plaza represents the first store in the western United States for Sixty-USA, the hot new specialty retailer.

The designers wished to maintain the pre-existing aesthetic, inspired by the design work of Vernor Panton, while evolving towards the futuristic and the organic. An important element was that the shopper's experience would change as she journeyed from the front of the store to the back.

Materials figured prominently in the design of the store, as did color and geometric shapes. Brightly lighted, shiny, color-saturated casework, pearlescent and vibrantly colored flooring and stainless steel mirror the buoyant 1960s style the retailer is after.

Forming a virtual connection with the mall's new metal high-tech bridge is an oversized sculptural stainless-steel polished mirror door with 12 conical portholes. Frameless, surrounded only by glass, the 7-by-12-foot door rotates on a central pivot, the result of a geometric calculation utilizing the rectangle and the circle, symbols of symmetry, order and simplicity.

The floor is divided into two different materials, colors and surfaces – one cold to the touch, but painted an ironic "hot" red; the other warmer, softer and lucid. LED lights, specially designed for the shallower mall floor, play across the borderline along the curve. Above, a serpentine shape pushes into the vinyl ceiling, then drops down in the middle of the space.

All this happens under a chaotic order of lights that perforate the ceiling, emulating a starry sky.

**CLIENT**
Sixty-USA, New York – Stefania Lapponi, visual coordinator

**DESIGN**
Borruso & Alessandro Design, Venice, Calif. – Giorgio Borruso, principal; Tiziana Alessandro, Elizabeth Chang, designers

**EXECUTIVE ARCHITECT**
PBWS Architects, Pasadena, Calif. – Fred Wesley, principal-in-charge; Rebecca Thompson, designer; Mark Smeaton, project architect

**GENERAL CONTRACTOR**
Sneden & Bowers Inc., Santa Ana, Calif.

**SUPPLIERS**
Zone One, New York (audio system); Fabric Wallcraft, Anaheim, Calif. (ceiling); Buzzoni SRL, Rovigo, Italy (furniture and fixtures); Lonseal, Carson, Calif. (soft flooring); Floor Systems, Anaheim, Calif. (flooring); Special-T Lighting, Burbank, Calif. (LED floor lighting); Bartco Lighting, Huntington Beach, Calif., Prudential Lighting Products, Los Angeles, RSA Lighting, Chatsworth, Calif. (ceiling lighting); Buzzoni SRL, Rovigo, Italy, SignQuest, Culver City, Calif. (signage and graphics); Chino Glass, Chino, Calif., PRL Glass Systems, City of Industry, Calif. (stainless-steel door); Eventscape, Toronto (fitting rooms)

**PHOTOGRAPHY**
Benny Chan/Fotoworks, Los Angeles

# Coach

Tokyo

*Michael Neumann Architecture, New York*

For Coach's first flagship in Japan, the challenge was to architecturally reinforce a classic American brand, but in a modern, style-savvy environment. The spirit of the store that resulted evoked the 1940s, post-war modernism of New York, and Coach's roots.

The two-story, 5400-square-foot store on a prominent corner in Tokyo's Ginza district is a limestone box with a white, glowing interior. A dramatic overhanging soffit sets off a 16-foot display window of ultra-clear museum glass (the largest glass panels ever installed in Tokyo). A monumental display wall and travertine staircase create the impression that customers occupy the front window. The shopper in the street, the mannequins in the front window and the customers inside the store interact within the same visual space.

Over the entry, back-lit glass in a mahogany-colored powdercoated frame evokes Coach gift boxes.

On the ground floor, the walnut stair wall becomes an elongated display area, with multiple glowing white display boxes offset by the dark wood. The rear feature wall shows the exterior limestone wrapping inside the store, punctuated by square display vitrines. Display tables are white-washed maple, white powdercoated tubular base and museum-glass tops.

Flooring is unfilled Persian white travertine in an ashlar pattern. The staircase is flanked on one side by a 19-foot-high wall of horizontally coursed limestone and a wall of walnut paneling. Handrails are solid walnut held by stainless-steel escutcheons embossed with a contrasting Coach signature "C" pattern.

**CLIENT**
Coach Store Design & Visual Merchandising, New York – Reed Krakoff, president/executive creative director; Patrick Wade, senior vp, global visual merchandising and store design; Michael Fernbacher, divisional vp, store design worldwide; Karin Cole, divisional vp, visual merchandising creative worldwide; Peter White, senior manager, international store design; Joy Bruder, director of visual merchandising, international and wholesale; Julie McGinnis, director, design services; John Gunter, director, visual merchandising, Japan; Chris Amplo, director, store operations, Japan; Kyoko Hasagawa, manager, visual merchandising, international; Greg Caputo, senior manager, retail and visual design

**DESIGN**
Michael Neumann Architecture, New York – Michael Neumann, principal; Jay Camelo, project manager; Jason DePierre, Tracy Look Hong, Alexander Olsen, Talin Rudy, project team

**OUTSIDE DESIGN CONSULTANTS**
Sato Facilities Consultants Inc., Tokyo (project management) – Takayoshi Sato, president; Ryuso Kiri, senior consulting manager; Tsugio Kurosawa, consulting manager; Worktech, Tokyo (lighting design) – Atushi Kaneda, president; Mie Noto, Akira Saito, lighting designers

**GENERAL CONTRACTOR**
Shimizu Corp., Tokyo

**SUPPLIER**
Soars Space Produce, Tokyo (fixtures, furniture)

**PHOTOGRAPHY**
Nacasa & Partners, Tokyo

AMERICAN
SUMMER
COACH

# Duty Free Shops
Buenos Aires, Argentina

*Point Design, New York*

Duty Free Shops in Buenos Aires' Ezeiza International Airport was intended to represent a bold new direction, creating dramatic retail environments to attract travelers to a rich selection of merchandise.

As created by Point Design (New York), the architecture of the 17,000-square-foot space in the International Departures concourse retains a traditional open floorplan while, at the same time, offering discrete shopping experiences in carefully designed areas.

International travelers enter the shops through the jewelry/fine watch area, leading to the intimacy of the perfume/fragrance shop. This area features an uplit floor inlaid with river-hewn pebbles.

As the traveler moves through each of the 13 shops, the mood changes. Areas such as gourmet food/wine/cigars are playful, using mosaic finishes and a loosely patterned vinyl floor tile. Suspended wood beams and industrial lighting help organize the food space.

While each area is distinctive, Point Design also selected finishes – and a neutral carpet and cherrywood floors –  to help bring cohesiveness to the entire space. Sisal carpets surrounded by pristine white walls tie the diverse elements together.

**CLIENT**
Interbaires S.A., Buenos Aires, Argentina – Alejandro Basile, principal-in-charge

**DESIGN**
Point Design, New York – Diego Garay, president; Lois Bruno, director; Leo Lotopolsky, project director; Brigida Squazzi, job captain; Lola Arenaza, graphics; Leandro Artigala, Mariana Silverman, Walter Mantegazza, Maria Bruno, Daniel Solessio, Marcelo Lopez, designers

**GENERAL CONTRACTOR:**
Rada Elly, Buenos Aires

**OUTSIDE DESIGN CONSULTANT**
Pablo Pizzarro, Buenos Aires (lighting design)

**SUPPLIERS**
Philips, Buenos Aires (audio/visual); Armstrong, Buenos Aires (ceiling); Maharam, Hauppauge, N.Y., Wolf Gordon, New York, Richter Group, New York (fabrics); Taddei, Buenos Aires, Recouso, Buenos Aires (fixturing); Armstrong, Buenos Aires, Innovative Marble, Hauppauge, N.Y. (flooring); Nuchi, Buenos Aires (furniture); H.B. Diseño, Buenos Aires (graphics); Reggiani, New York (lighting); Wilsonart, Buenos Aires, Abet, Buenos Aires (laminates); Maharam, Hauppauge, N.Y., Wolf Gordon, New York, Richter Group, New York (wallcoverings)

**PHOTOGRAPHY**
Daniela Macadden, Buenos Aires

BURBERRY
BURBERRY

# Neutrogena

Northridge Fashion Center, Northridge, Calif.

*TL Horton Design, Grapevine, Texas*

For its first shopping center kiosk, Neutrogena Corp. (Los Angeles) wanted a professional retail environment that reflected its clean image and clear brand identity.

Its 10-by-24-foot kiosk had three main objectives: to provide the customer with a personalized skincare analysis; to educate the customer; and to sell products.

At the center of the kiosk are two skincare analysis stations, each with a set of cameras and lights (partially concealed by a frosted acrylic enclosure). Photos are taken of the customer's skin and displayed on a countertop-mounted monitor. The customer is given a printout of her photos and a regimen to solve problems.

Directly behind the skincare analysis is a self-service product wall, with products easily visible and accessible.

One of the main design challenges was to create display space for the entire Neutrogena product line. So, at the front of the kiosk, cosmetics are located in glass cases, lighted by cabinet lighting and decorative pendants.

Since the flow of water is used in the company's advertising as a symbol for purity, a waterwall is incorporated into the back wall of the kiosk. Feature products can be highlighted by a graphic placed on the waterwall and backlit glass display cases on each side.

The header of the kiosk has an amber glow, the color of Neutrogena's famous cleansing bar.

**CLIENT**
Neutrogena Corp., Los Angeles

**DESIGN**
TL Horton Design, Grapevine, Texas – Garry Cohn, creative director; Stan Zalenski, senior vp; Rob McCoy, account executive; Erin Knoettgen-Nap, designer

**SUPPLIERS**
Gyford Productions, Reno, Nev., Mammen Glass, Irving, Texas, Riddle Enterprises, Garland, Texas, Stylmark, Minneapolis (fixturing); Design Within Reach, San Francisco (furniture); Innovative Lighting, Irving, Texas, Nu-Tech Lighting, Newtown, Pa. (lighting); Kenmark (Abet Laminati), Dallas, Wilsonart Intl., Chicago (laminates)

**PHOTOGRAPHY**
Joe Aker, Houston

Neutrogena

# Pandini's

Lehigh University Student Center,
Bethlehem, Pa.

*Connor Architecture, Arlington, Mass.*

The challenge: to create a new retail branded pizza concept with an architectural image embodying quality, variety, freshness and taste. Seeking to avoid the typical college pizza joint syndrome, the Pandini's concept was to inspire customers to have a memorable, enthusiastic dining experience.

Circles, ovals and rectangles are collaged together to create a necklace of menu-driven stations. Each station is assigned a distinct shape, palette of finishes and unique iconography. The resulting "zoning" of stations allows each menu component to have its own territory and display format, featuring its products in the most appealing light.

Red, yellow and orange-toned linoleum radiates from the circular copper and aluminum pizza counter. A crown of brushed aluminum rays pierce the round soffit above, serving to reinforce the oven's sun-like image. An abstract trellis of steel and mahogany helps capture the garden quality of the salad station. And a check pattern of glazed ceramic tile in Tuscan red and mustard yellow animates the pasta kitchen's back wall.

The dining room is an extension of the kitchen. A mix of multi-colored banquettes with metallic finials and freestanding maple tables provides a variety of seating options. A metal and maple canopy is suspended above. Maple and cherry finishes, highlighted by suspended glass pendants and warm Renaissance portraits, create intimacy.

**CLIENT**
Lehigh University, Bethlehem, Pa. – Patricia Chase; Sodexho, Gaithersburg, Md. – Husein Ktabwalla, Denis Karbach, Holly Smith, brand design group

**DESIGN**
Connor Architecture, Arlington, Mass. – Mark Connor, principal; Robert Weire, associate; Jayson Herzog, designer

**GENERAL CONTRACTOR**
Atlantic Equipment Specialist, Danville, Pa.

**SUPPLIERS**
Atlas Carpets, Los Angeles, Forbo, Hazelton, Pa. (flooring); Juno Lighting, Des Plaines, Ill., Lightolier, Fall River, Mass. (lighting); Lamin-Art, Elk Grove Village, Ill., Nevamar, Odenton, Md., Panolam, Shelton, Conn. (laminates); Benjamin Moore, Montvale, N.J., Dal-Tile Corp. Dallas, (wallcoverings)

**PHOTOGRAPHY**
Anton Grassl, Boston

SALAD
Old World Style, New World Flavor
Panchnis
PIZZA
Labretti

# Holt's Café,
# Holt Renfrew

Toronto

*II BY IV Design Associates, Toronto*

The restaurant inside Holt Renfrew's renovated Bloor Street store in Toronto was not simply to give shoppers a place to eat. It was also to be a showcase for the upscale retailer's fashionable home decor products.

Creating a bold, chic statement was not helped by the fact that the entrances to the restaurant were squeezed in between the lingerie department and a small rear elevator lobby. Both access points were treated with deep marble-faced portals topped with simple backlit signage letters. A small selection of important accessories is also displayed on a 12-foot-long, low elliptical table in glossy white MDF, its seamless acid-etched glass top underlit and topped with display risers in stainless steel and clear glass.

Just beyond the entrance, above tiny floor lights, a group of custom "stiletto" tables are positioned, with a matching group in the rear. Between is a long center line of fixtures separating the primary display wall from the bar and dining area, which overlooks the street below.

The 31-foot bar is centered against the window wall, flanked by dining seating. Primary materials include glass, stainless steel and pearl-finished and gloss-white MDF and white glazed tiles. The long bar is faced with high-gloss glass building cladding material. Translucent film is sandwiched between glass layers on the display wall's back panel, with simple fluorescent fixtures at rear top and bottom, emitting a radiant uniform glow.

**CLIENT**

Holt Renfrew, Toronto – Andrew Jennings, Bob Tonk, David Battle, Natalie Penno, Corbin Tomaszeski, Peter Moore

**DESIGN**

II BY IV Design Associates Inc., Toronto – Keith Rushbrook, Dan Menchions, Grace Eng, Andy Verheil, Allan Tse, Jenny Lee, Azen Barker Jones

**ARCHITECT**

Young & Wright Associates, Toronto

**GENERAL CONTRACTOR**

Pickett & Associates, Toronto

**SUPPLIERS**

Benjamin Moore, Toronto (paint); Architectural Systems Inc., New York, Olympia Tile, Toronto (flooring); Italdoor & Woodworking Ltd., Toronto (doors); Häefele, Mississauga, Ont. (door hardware); Vast Interiors, Concord, Ont. (glass, custom tables); Matrix Custom Metals, Brampton, Ont. (railings/screens/grillwork); Kiosk, Toronto (dining chairs); Litemore, Toronto (light fixtures); Maharam, Toronto (fabrics); Vienna Upholstery, Toronto (upholstery); Copacetic Woodworking, Toronto, Ashford Interiors, Mississauga, Ont., Joseph Yanuzello, Toronto (architectural woodworking); Wilcox Sign Co., Toronto (signage)

**PHOTOGRAPHY**

David Whittaker, Toronto

# Wild Oats

Marina Shopping Center, Long Beach, Calif.

*Design Forum, Dayton, Ohio*

Wild Oats (Boulder, Colo.) is a chain of grocery stores dedicated to quality organic products. For its new prototype store in Long Beach, Calif., there were three primary objectives: an approachable interior that would build a bridge from the traditional grocery store to the emerging trend toward organic living; a distinct look to communicate the Wild Oats personality; and a design that could be efficiently rolled out.

The new look and store layout incorporate elements of the traditional grocery, welcoming the conventional shopper who may not have shopped in a natural or organic food store in the past. A deli, pizzeria and sushi take-out area offer prepared foods and sampling opportunities. The Natural Living department combines different graphics, signage and lower-profile shelving to create a service-friendly environment for shoppers of vitamins, supplements and natural body care products.

For its distinct look, the design team decided on "funky elegance," communicating style and personality through its signage package. Quick-read graphics are designed to encourage exploration of additional product offerings while helping shoppers navigate the store.

The design works around the existing interior elements so that any current store can be updated without major remodeling. Standardized materials and finishes provide the necessary building blocks to efficiently expand into additional markets with a common store format.

**CLIENT**

Wild Oats Markets Inc., Boulder, Colo. – Tracy Lindsey, director, plan development; Steve Cable, senior director, new store development; Abel Villacorta, creative director; Terry Maloy, chief marketing officer; Mike Kramer, senior director, construction; Jay Brown, plan development manager; Bud Anderson, plan development manager; Robin Nick, director, advertising and marketing

**DESIGN**

Design Forum, Dayton, Ohio – Bruce Dybvad, president; Meg Kenney, account manager; Emily Shapiro, graphic designer; Donny Victorianus, senior environmental designer; Jason Walker, resource specialist

**ARCHITECT**

MCG Architecture, Pasadena, Calif.

**GENERAL CONTRACTOR**

RAS Builders, Englewood, Colo.

**SUPPLIERS**

Abolite, Carrollton, Texas; Juno Lighting, Des Plaines, Ill., LBL Lighting, Chicago Heights, Ill. (lighting); S&G Mfg. Group, Hilliard, Ohio (metal panel); Benjamin Moore, Montvale, N.J. (paint finishes); Kramer Graphics, Dayton, Ohio (signage); ArCom Fabrics, Orangeburg, N.Y. (vinyl); Dal-Tile, Dallas (wall tile); Sherwin-Williams, Cleveland (wood stain)

**PHOTOGRAPHY**

Jamie Padgett, Padgett & Co., Chicago

Wine
grapes for grown-ups
Beer
tasty traditional old-world brews

WILD OATS
NATURAL MARKETPLACE
discover
taste
nourish
share
celebrate

Natural Living
nourish · soul · mind · body & spirit
mind · body & spirit
Spirit
Natural Knowledge
Wild
eat well · bon appetit
Body
children's health
women's health
natural beauty
herbal supplements
hair care

Wild Oasis
elixirs for the spirit
Natural Knowledge
Wild Cafe
ZOE
EXTRA VIRGIN OLIVE OIL

## Gelson's

New Paseo Colorado Shopping Center,
Pasadena, Calif.

*King Design Intl., Eugene, Ore.*

The credo for this new Southern California supermarket was: "It's not creative unless it translates to the real world – and works!"

The store itself is a combination of Southern California art deco sensibility and the successful presentation of produce and food products. Three entrances – one from the lower lobby to the underground parking garage – lead into the space. The challenging footprint is narrow and deep, with a dog-leg extension and ceilings that vary from 11 to 14 feet. Structural columns also added to the design problems.

However, by using floating ceilings and adding architectural features and murals to the columns, designers were able to incorporate the required merchandise layout.

The retailer requested that the interior design tie in with the local, upscale community. Deco colored laminates and paints and ceramic tiles provide a variety of finishes. Special departmental signage and architectural features and graphics, all in the art deco style, define each space and product line. Custom chandeliers over the entrance, check-out and service areas and fireside seating add upscale aspects.

**CLIENT**
Gelson's Markets, Encino, Calif. – Robert Stiles, president; Drew Randolph, store construction

**DESIGN**
King Design Intl., Eugene, Ore. – William Volm, president; Becky Phegley, project manager; Christopher Studach, design director; Mike Hopper, designer

**ARCHITECT**
MCG Architecture, Pasadena, Calif.

**GENERAL CONTRACTOR**
A.J. Podelford & Son Inc., Cerritos, Calif.

**OUTSIDE DESIGN CONSULTANT**
Designing in Light, Pasadena, Calif.

**SUPPLIERS**
Celotex Corp., Tampa (ceiling); Dal-Tile, Dallas (flooring); Nevamar, Odenton, Md., Formica, Cincinnati, Panolam, Shelton, Conn. (laminates)

**PHOTOGRAPHY**
Courtesy of King Design Intl., Eugene, Ore.

# York Event Theatre

Toronto

*II BY IV Design Associates Inc., Toronto*

York Event Theatre (Toronto), an entertainment consortium, focuses on adaptive re-use projects, converting movie houses into hot venues. For this particular project, they wanted to meet an explicit market need – a fashionable, modern setting, complete with functional and stylish amenities, for planners of both corporate and social special occasions.

Illuminated effects play an important role in both the exterior and interior aspects of the concept. Fiberoptics, illuminated signage boxes and a large video board were used to add color, light and movement to the theater's monolithic concrete slab face, creating a beacon-like street presence. Chrome-clad entryway columns reflect that radiance and the light pouring from the deep light-lined entryway.

Glass doors lead to a large lobby sparkling with illuminated display niches filled with glass sculptures, white terrazo flooring, metal wall paneling and custom glass drop chandeliers. A mirrored exterior and illuminated water features enhance the drama of an existing glass elevator.

Throughout the facility, illuminated sandblasted glass and acrylic bars and back-bar features and mirrored walls, ceilings and display niches create a play of light and shadow on wood-block wall features, thick full-height drapery and stainless-steel and glass decorative details.

The project also won a Special Award for Most Innovative Concept.

**CLIENT**
York Event Theatre, Toronto

**DESIGN**
II BY IV Design Associates Inc., Toronto – Dan Menchions, Keith Rushbrook, Andy Verhiel, Yvonne Ho, Jenny Lee, Allan Tse, Misa Torii, Tanya Lukezic

**ARCHITECT**
Lorne Rose Architect Inc., Toronto

**GENERAL CONTRACTOR**
Dewbourne Developments, Toronto

**SUPPLIERS**
Tappatec, Mississauga, Ont. (custom carpet); R&R Staging, Toronto (drapery); Z&D Finishes, Toronto (millwork); 3M Canada, London, Ont. (window film); Jeff Goodman Studio, Toronto (custom glass chandelier); Ace Glass, Toronto (doors/mirrors/glass guards); Signage Systems, Brompton, Ont. (signage); Signs of Change, Toronto (event room wall panels); Olympia Tile, Toronto (washroom/ kitchen); Serious Stainless, Toronto (metalwork); Benjamin Moore, Toronto (paint); Principessa Intl. Marble & Granite, Toronto (bar and washroom counters/lobby feature); Quarella Inc., Woodbridge, Ont. (lobby flooring); General Wood & Veneers Ltd., Mississauga, Ont. (wood veneer); Quality Upholstery, Woodbridge, Ont. (custom furniture); Contract Supply Corp., Mississauga, Ont. (dining chairs and stools); Triden Distributors Ltd., Toronto (fabric); Lightolier, Toronto (lighting fixtures)

**PHOTOGRAPHY**
David Whittaker, Toronto

# Station K

Toronto

*Perennial Inc., Toronto*

In 2001, faced with the rapid growth of competitive forms of communications delivery, government-owned Canada Post undertook a large-scale repositioning, transforming its traditional post office into a retail operation.

Station K was meant to be a "connections store," the center that brings people, business and government together. Because it's government-owned and has more than 4000 corporate and 2800 dealer outlets across the country, it's in a unique position to dominate its core offering – sending and receiving – and deliver key value-added products and services in heritage and culture, government services, small-business services (box rental, direct-mail fulfillment, etc.) and money services (money orders, authentication, etc.).

The space was expanded to 2400 square feet and zoned so customers could browse at their own pace, or get in and out quickly if they wished. The Postal Services zone faces the entry, with three cashwrap counters to serve customers with stamps, shipping advice or money services.

Each customer offering was assigned a decor color (paint finishes, wall graphics, signage and communications): Postal Services was coded red; Small Business was bright orange; Government Services was assigned blue; and Gifts & Collectibles, Stationery and a special Kid's Zone were coded green.

Unifying this is a consistent approach to graphics and communications across all departments. Bold images, banners, wayfinding and in-store signage reinforce the character of the brand while guiding customers to the appropriate product or service.

**CLIENT**

Canada Post Corp., Ottawa – Susan Jahudka, project manager; Tom Froggatt, visual merchandising director; Sheila Beehler-Walsh, Catherine Riggins, marketing managers; Hala Hawa, design manager; Karine Lessard, Martin Quesnel, Alain Sigouin, Jennifer Watters, designers; Jan Mullet, David Wilson, construction

**DESIGN**

Perennial Inc., Toronto – Chris Lund, president; Joe Jackman, partner-in-charge; Joanne Balles, managing director; Jill Flaherty, project manager; Jana Makalic, director, environmental design; Steven Commisso, Mark Matla, designers

**ARCHITECT**

John Moses Architect, Oshawa, Ont.

**GENERAL CONTRACTOR**

MHPM Project Managers Inc., Burlington, Ont.

**SUPPLIERS**

CHUM Satellite Services, Toronto (audio/visual); ALU, Toronto, EurOptimum Display, Toronto, J&J Display, Mississauga, Ont. (fixturing); Armstrong, Montreal (flooring); Plessis, Plessisville, Que., Tricas, Hull, Que. (furniture); les Freres Proulx, Ottawa, Ont. (graphics); Arborite, Lasalle, Que., Formica Canada, Saint-Jean-Sur-Richelieu, Que., Simtab Panneaux Neos, Laval, Que. (laminates); Leader Mfg., Toronto, Tenaquip, Ste-Anne-De-Bellevue, Que. (props/decoratives); TransCanada Signs, Anjou, Que. (signage)

**PHOTOGRAPHY**

Richard Desmarais, Ottawa

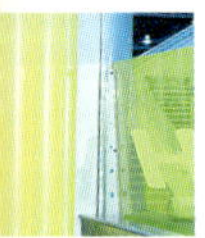

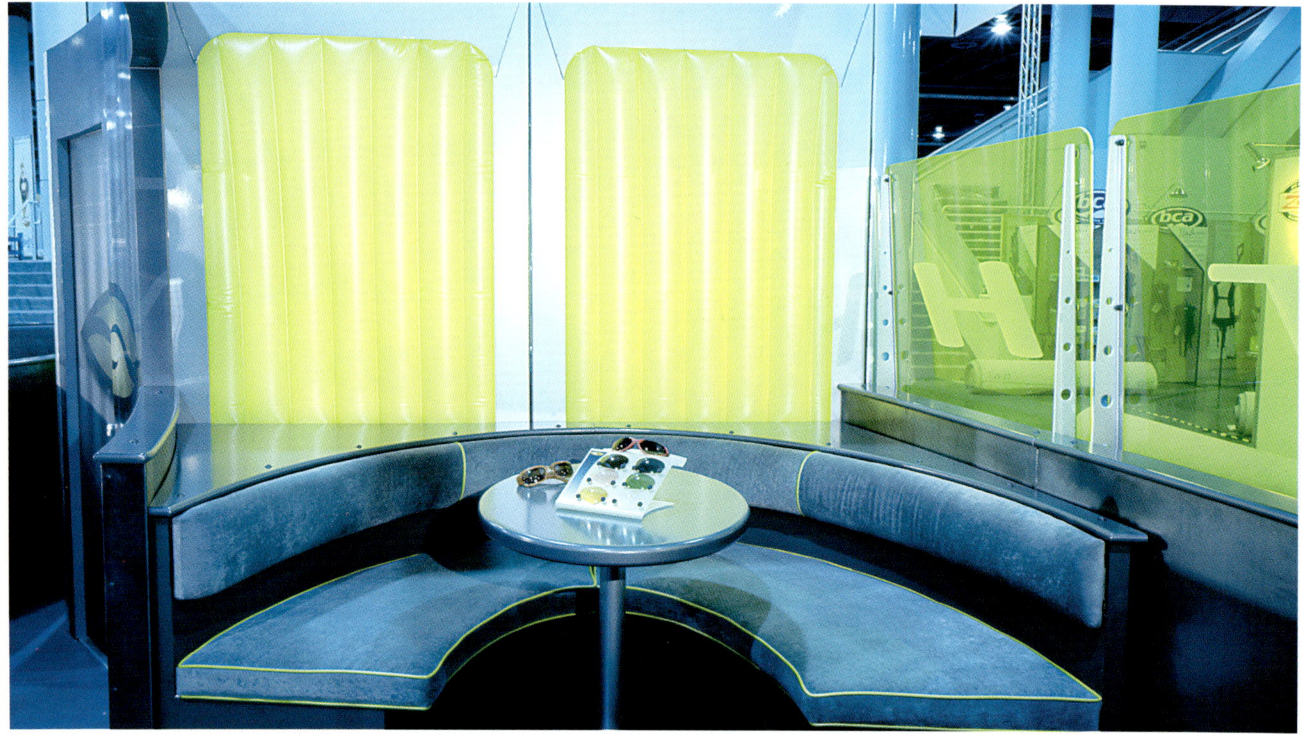

# Smith Exhibit Showroom

SIA Tradeshow, Las Vegas Convention Center

*Utility Inc., Seattle*

Smith Sport Optics (Ketchum, Idaho) makes things like goggles, ski poles and sunglasses for the active outdoors market. Because it feels its market is dominated by image and exposure, it assigned Utility Inc. (Seattle) to create a booth for the annual SIA (SnowSport Industries America) show in Las Vegas that embodied and was emblematic of the company's straightforward, strong and steady design sensibility approach, and its role as leader rather than follower in its industry.

The booth would then become part of the company's showroom, and the model for its vendor shops.

Envisioned as a "nightclub for buyers" that attracts and breeds energy, the environment fused interactivity with inspiration. An exoskeleton of aluminum panels has inter-changeable wall skins. Use of materials included luminescent inflatable chartreuse wall panels, neon acrylics and proprietary oiled and waxed patina steel finishes.

Heavily laquered bar countertops are illuminated from above and from within with custom-designed lighting to create a glowing product stage, juxtaposed by the intimate green suede cushioned lounge booths.

**CLIENT**
Smith Sport Optics, Ketchum, Idaho – Ned Post, owner; Kerry Marumoto, vp, marketing; Stephanie Carlson, director of exhibits

**DESIGN**
Utility Inc., Seattle – Todd Jacobsen, principal; Carm Pierce, senior designer

**SUPPLIER**
Utility Inc., Seattle (fixturing, furniture, graphics, props/decoratives, signage)

**PHOTOGRAPHY**
Mark Knight, Austin, Tex.

# Levi's Cinch

London

*Checkland Kindleysides, Leicester, U.K.*

A rope-like, 750-foot-long red "thread" wends its way through the redesigned Levi's Cinch store on London's Newburgh Street. To Checkland Kindleysides (Leicester, U.K.), this design element – made of painted twine – was meant to serve as a "sinuous signature" for the Levi's brand, since it evokes the stitching of the company's trademark jeans. (The thread also serves as a navigation aid through the space, which is a collection of small rooms spread over three floors.)

"The Levi's brand has continually evolved since the 1850s," says Jeff Kindleysides, the design firm's principal-in-charge for the project, "and the concept behind the thread was to symbolize this lineage and continuity."

Levi's merchandise hangs from the oversized "thread," which runs along the space's white walls. This setup "elevates and showcases the product as the space's 'hero,' " says Kindleysides. But while the walls are designed to have a sleek, modern look, other surfaces within the store reflect Levi's long history. For example, copper was used in the flooring and fascia, and denim was installed in the stair treads.

**CLIENT**
Levi Strauss & Co., San Francisco – Henry Barnes, European store designer; Rosanna Iacono, premium brand director; Gary Harvey, clothing design team creative director

**DESIGN**
Checkland Kindleysides, Leicester, U.K. – Jeff Kindleysides, principal-in-charge; Jason West, design director; Russell Ashdown, Guy Tabberer, designers; Lucy Ashley, project manager

**SUPPLIER**
Checkland Kindleysides, Leicester, U.K. (ceilings, fixturing, signage)

**PHOTOGRAPHY**
Adrian Wilson, Cheshire, U.K.

## Palm Café

Santa Clara, Calif.

*B&N Industries, San Carlos, Calif.*

Palm Solutions (Milpitas, Calif.) wanted a cost-effective way to bring its personal hand-held computers and accessories to a retail audience. The company, which had been selling its products online, found the answer not in a full store design but in an open café-like space featuring a series of tables, stations, kiosks and signage.

"The devices themselves are small, so you don't really need a whole store," says Kevin McPhee, image director at B&N Industries (San Carlos, Calif.), who worked with Palm Solutions on the fixture design.

So designers decided to group several of the fixtures together to create a freestanding kiosk area, called the Palm Café, that could easily fit into the common areas of malls and airports "and keep costs down," says McPhee. "It also created an environment where people could freely walk in and out of the space and be able to interact with the live devices."

The space is made up of B&N's Sorbetti freestanding floor fixture system. Each fixture unit is 36 inches in diameter and 9 feet tall and features an internal power source for running the devices, the lighting and the security system.

To distinguish Palm's different product categories, designers used two color schemes for the fixtures: silver units for Palm professional business products; and orange for Palm everyday products, geared toward families and recreational uses. Signage and graphics related to each brand message and target audience hang from fixture poles.

Accessories are located at the main cashwrap or in clear acrylic boxes mounted on the fixture poles.

To enhance visibility in crowded settings, each fixture has an illuminated Palm logo mounted atop the center fixture pole. Fluorescent tube lights (from Hera Lighting, Norcross, Ga.) illuminate the graphics, while smaller Tolomeo lamps (from Artemide, Farmingdale, N.Y.) hang above the work counters.

**CLIENT**
Palm Solutions, Milpitas, Calif. – Kanwal Sharma, head of retail development and special projects

**DESIGN**
B&N Industries, San Carlos, Calif. – Brad Somberg, president; Kevin McPhee, planner, designer and manager in-charge; Pirkko Lucchesi, project manager

**GENERAL CONTRACTOR**
Superior Construction, Campbell, Calif.

**OUTSIDE DESIGN CONSULTANT**
Hera Lighting, Norcross, Ga.

**SUPPLIERS**
B&N Industries, San Carlos, Calif. (fixturing, graphics design); BT Mancini, Milpitas, Calif. (flooring); Design Within Reach, San Francisco (furniture); HN Lockwood, Redwood City, Calif. (graphics); Artemide, Farmingdale, N.Y. (lighting); Formica, Warren, N.J. (laminates); JP Digital, Mountain View, Calif. (signage); Viewrite Mfg., Daly City, Calif. (acrylic work)

**PHOTOGRAPHY**
Michael Skott, Orcas Island, Wash.

The Point Is It's Only $99
e point is it's easy.
From Your
Palm Handheld
To Your Desktop:
Transfer
And Update
With Ease.
Beam
Information.
palm

TUNGSTEN T
PROBLEM SOLVED
palm
One-Hand Navigation.
Expandable.
Compact Design.
Transfer.
Connect.
Mobile.
Connected.
Print.
Share.
bluefish

palm
the point is: it's easy.
Fantastic Color.
Fantastic Value.
m130
HotSync.
m130
palm

E*TRADING RETAIL SPACES

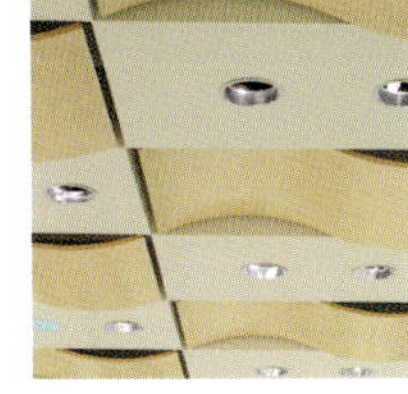
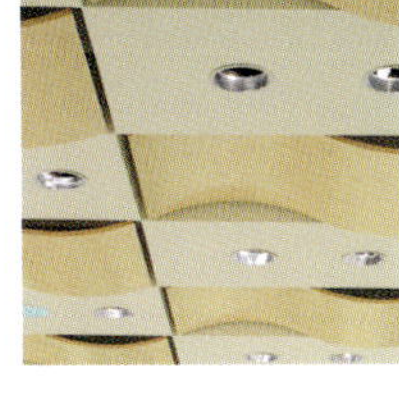

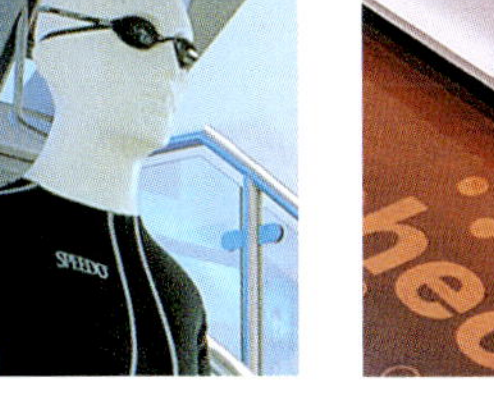

# 5

STORES
AND
RETAIL
SPACES

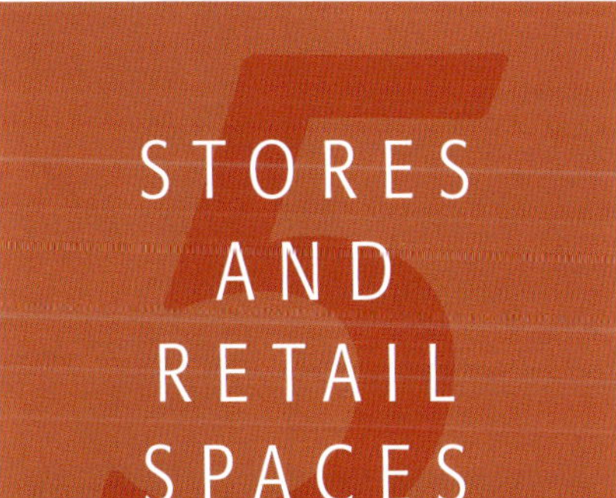
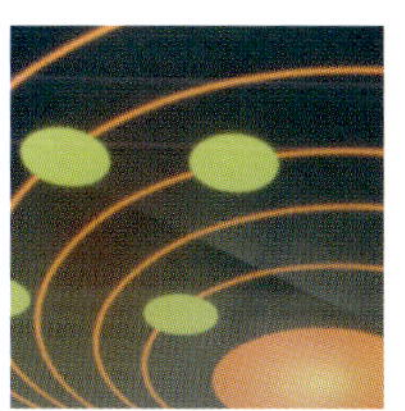

# E*TRADE

Madison Avenue, New York

*Retail Planning Associates, Columbus, Ohio*

The design objective was to open a financial services superstore "to give customers value-added financial services and educational content in a high-tech, high-touch experience."

E*TRADE had a list of functional requirements: a state-of-the-art trading room, club-like VIP area and an interactive educational seminar center. Most important, the entire retail facility had to be as customer-friendly and easy to navigate as E*TRADE's web site. Or, as RPA vp and program officer Pat Heinzman said, the primary goal was "to capture the overall brand essence of E*TRADE within the space."

RPA interpreted the E*TRADE brand essence as one of high-end services, high-tech sophistication, dependability, confidentiality and interactivity. So the space was designed around more than 100 15-square-foot flatscreen monitors and a collection of shiny powdercoated metal "cobra" pods for private transactions.

To satisfy investors at all levels, the four-story space veers from the cellar – where investors work at 50 individual stations – to a Club E*TRADE on the mezzanine for private, comfortable, high-end financial management in a plush setting of overstuffed chairs and tables with their own laptop computers.

On the top level is a retail store filled with E*TRADE branded products (from T-shirts to Kenneth Cole leather goods), a library and a Mangia café.

A spiral staircase snakes up through the center of the store, wrapped around a central column painted in E*TRADE purple.

Windowed glass walls on both Madison and 55th Street allow the store's energy, sleekness and color and motion to project out into the Midtown New York night.

**CLIENT**

E*TRADE, San Francisco – Christo Cotsakos, chairman and ceo; Jerry Gramaglia, president and coo; Michael Sievert, chief marketing officer; Tim Heard, vp, retail marketing; Sean Millis, facilitator of change; Bobbi Clemens, manager, event marketing; Erika Szychowski, manager, event marketing; Brian Calnon, director, real world marketing; Robert Monteleone, director, operations and sales; Eddie Dombrower, vp, executive producer DFM; Don Vielleux, executive producer DFM; J.P. Asperin, group design manager, multimedia; John Garcia, senior systems engineer; Lloyd Terry, lead network engineer; Lisa Rogers, project manager; Barbara Myers, project manager; Scott Stevenson, recruitment

**DESIGN**

Retail Planning Associates, Columbus, Ohio – Pat Heinzman, executive program officer; Karen Rumora, environmental designer; Tonya Schloemer, program manager; Paul Hamilton, senior environmental designer; David Spurbeck, senior documentation specialist; Johnna Castle, design resource manager; Carla Charvat, graphic designer; Shelly Schnabel, art director; Dana Fleming, merchandiser/planner; Kurt Shade, senior environmental designer; Mark Holman, senior lighting designer; Perry Kotick, senior lighting designer

**SUPPLIERS**

Mannington Commercial, Calhoun, Ga. (carpet); Dal-Tile, Dallas (tile); Amtico Intl., Atlanta (flooring and vinyl tile); Sherwin Williams, Kendallville, Ind. (paint); Nevamar, Odenton, Md., Formica Corp., Cincinnati, Pioneer Plastics, Auburn, Maine (laminates); Bam Bam Design, Pasadena, Calif., Rimex Metals, Edison, N.J., Matrix Fixtures, Hastings on Hudson, N.Y. (special finishes); Johnsonite, Chagrin Falls, Ohio (wallbase); Permagrain, Newton Square, Pa. (wood)

**PHOTOGRAPHY**

Whitney Cox, New York

INVESTING
E*TRADE Securities
E*TRADE
center
new york city
E*TRADE
center
new york city
nyse          price down
BYLS
HYLAND SOFTWARE SERVICES
INC
45.25    -4.98%
Volume: 596,300
May 21, 2001 6:01 PM
nasdaq          percent up
BCOR
MEXICO COMPUTER CORPORATION
7.45    +6.543%
Volume: 55,207,800
May 21, 2001 5:00 PM
nasdaq          percent up
BCOR
MEXICO COMPUTER CORPORATION
7.45    +6.543%
Volume: 55,207,800
May 21, 2001 5:00 PM
nasdaq          most actives
ERICY
LM ERICSSON TELEPHONE CO
ADR
7.35    +6.37%
Volume: 34,223,100
May 21, 2001 4:00 PM
daq          most actives
ICY
RICSSON TELEPHONE CO
+6.37%
me: 34,223,100
4:00 PM
NYSE COMPOSITE
INDEX
663.56
+0.98%
May 21, 2001 6:51 PM

mobile
E*TRADE
center
by
AETHER
Keeping you
connected
and productive.

mobile
E*TRADE
center
by
AETHER

## Woolworths

Gateway Shopping Center, Kwazulu-Natal,
Republic of South Africa

*Woolworths Ltd., Capetown, Republic of South Africa*

The 150-store chain fights competition throughout Africa and the Middle East, and so is constantly looking to innovate its stores. Its brief to the internal design team for its new shopping center store in South Africa was to create a fresh new look that would "pleasantly surprise but not alienate its existing, somewhat traditional, customer base and at the same time attract new customers."

No problem! The 54,000-square-foot store was made to look much bigger by the use of clean white ceilings, uncluttered floor space and simple display units. The store was designed as a white box, enabling the in-store staff to change colors and visuals to match the changing seasons. Most of the visuals are back-lit to provide a glow, and the lighting levels have been brought down to achieve the calm, almost intimate effect the designers were after.

Nowhere is this atmosphere more apparent than in the food section, designed to look and feel like a market. The floors are concrete, the fixtures brushed aluminum and there's also liberal use of dark-stained oak. The look is carried through to the wine shop.

**CLIENT**
Woolworths, Capetown, Republic of South Africa

**SUPPLIERS**
Al-Clad Interiors, Johannesburg, South Africa (fixtures); Quad Africa, Johannesburg, South Africa (lighting); Wilsonart Intl., Temple, Texas (laminates); Hollywood Displays, Johannesburg, South Africa (mannequins and forms); Fast Track Ceilings, Johannesburg, South Africa (ceilings)

**PHOTOGRAPHY**
Courtesy of Woolworth's, Capetown, Republic of South Africa

younger girls
1 - 8 yrs
just arrived

ora
life and freshness
foodmarket

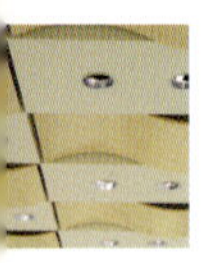

# Neiman Marcus

International Plaza, Tampa, Fla.

*Robert Young Associates, Dallas*

Neiman Marcus invaded western Florida with a classic Neiman's look – elegant and modernistic – through the filter of a casual Gulf Coast temperament.

Robert Young Associates (Dallas) created a clean, unobstructed space using simple geometric forms to delineate merchandise categories. Clear, cool colors frame merchandise within larger, neutral volumes. Celestory windows provide filtered daylight to the store's interior.

The design centerpiece of the store is the evening room in the women's department. Here, individual cabinets in cream lacquer feature shallow panels of gilded glass with an abstracted wave pattern and backgrounds of shagreen (a granular leather surface). A satin nickel grill outlines each cabinet.

In men's, cerused oak perimeters feature bright blue accents. Low walls in furnishings are capped with sinuous bands of blue glass mosaic tiles that snake across the top and drop down to the floor at the end panels.

Cosmetics is delineated by a raised ceiling whose sides are formed by deep, lighted slots. In the center is an elliptical plane bracketed by two crescent-shaped slots. The department's perimeters are linked to the larger architectural ideas of the store by crisp, rectangular merchandise slots, framed by thin bands of color set into larger white frames.

A wave theme, perhaps referencing the soft and gentle Gulf Coast waters, repeats throughout the store.

**CLIENT**
Neiman Marcus, Dallas – Collette Ventrone, vp, store planning and design; Ignaz Gorischek, vp, visual planning and design; Chris Lebamoff, director, store planning and design

**DESIGN**
Robert Young Associates, Dallas – Tom Herndon, ceo; Jeff Henderson, senior planner; Mike Wilkins, principal-in-charge; Chris Chavez, job captain; Bill Plaisance, senior designer

**ARCHITECT**
Diedrich/NBA, Atlanta

**OUTSIDE DESIGN CONSULTANT**
Integrated Lighting, West Lake Village, Calif.

**GENERAL CONTRACTOR**
Hoar Construction, Tampa

**SUPPLIERS**
Ripple Effects Inc., New York (ceilings); Donghia, New York, Bernhardt Design, Lenoir, N.C., The Knoll Group, New York, Pollack, New York, Gretchen Bellinger Inc., Cohoes, N.Y. (fabrics); Edron, Miami, Goebel Fixture Co., Hutchinson, Minn., Custom Architectural Woodworking, Phoenix, Dooge Veneers, Grand Rapids, Mich., American Burnishing, New York, Bisazza, Miami, Ventec Ltd., Chicago, Brookside Veneer, Cranbury, N.J. (fixturing); Constantine, Dalton, Ga., Shaw, Dalton, Ga., Invision Carpet Systems, Dalton, Ga., Atlas Carpet Mills, Los Angeles, Innovative Marble & Tile Inc., Hauppauge, N.Y., Scott Group Custom Carpets, Grand Rapids, Mich. (flooring); Sutherland, Dallas, J. Manheim Custom Furniture, Dallas, Donghia, New York, Dakota Jackson Inc., New York, J. Robert Scott, Inglewood, Calif., Bright Chair Co., Middleton, N.Y., Heltzer Inc., Chicago (furniture); Prescolite, San Leandro, Calif., Columbia Lighting, Spokane, Wash., Indy Lighting, Fishers, Ind. (lighting); Anya Larking Inc., New York, Maharam, New York, Donghia, New York, The Knoll Group, New York, Blumenthal Inc., Canaan, Conn., Southwest Progressive, Richardson, Texas (wallcoverings)

**PHOTOGRAPHY**
Paul Bielenberg, Los Angeles

# Essences

Rustan's Department Store,
Makati City, the Philippines

*Retail Planning Associates, Columbus, Ohio*

Rustan's is one of the major retailers in the Philippines, and its superstore adjacent to the Ayala Center in Makati City is one of the area's most upscale shopping destinations. But it wanted to grow its market, expanding its line of high-end cosmetics among Manila's young, trendy fashionistas.

Retail Planning Associates (Columbus, Ohio) responded by creating a shop with a lifestyle approach to body care and treatments, opening up the surroundings to suggest airiness, rest and liquidity.

The exterior is composed of three sides of seamless glass, drawing customers to the space through the bustle of cars, exhaust fumes and pedestrian traffic. The shop is meant to be a decompression zone of peace and relaxation. At night, the shop is a beacon, reflecting beckoning prisms of light.

Inside, the color white was used to promote well-being. The rear walls are back-lit to create the warm, inviting glow. Curvilinear shapes – in mirrors, column wraps, sofas and specialty fixtures – soften the environment.

Cosmetics is presented in open-sell fixturing, and tester stations were developed for makeup applications and demonstrations from visiting makeup artists. Lighting replicates daylight and also enhances the natural warmth of Filipinos' skin tones.

The relaxing centerpiece is a Tea Bar. Dropped-down residential-style pendant lighting was used to raise awareness and increase the comfort level. The retro-style furnishings, mimicking the comfort of a home's living room, were used to increase dwell time. Natural wood chairs are carved to fit body contours.

**CLIENT**
Rustan's Department Store, Manila, the Philippines

**DESIGN**
Retail Planning Associates, Columbus, Ohio – Peter McIlroy, partner, international services; Nicholas Baughman, senior studio officer; Jason Woods, associate merchandiser/planner; Paul Teeples, environmental designer; Johanna Castle, design resources manager; Dave Spurbeck, senior documentation specialist; Stephen Jay, retail strategist; Perry Kotick, senior lighting designer

**OUTSIDE DESIGN CONSULTANT**
Sonia Santiago Olivares and Associates, Manila, the Philippines

**SUPPLIERS**
E.C. Paulion, Manila, the Philippines (construction); Vigor Systems, Chachoengsao, Thailand (freestanding fixtures); J. Walters, Manila, the Philippines (graphics)

**PHOTOGRAPHY**
Philip Escudero, Manila, the Philippines

essense

essenses

essenses
essenses
essenses
essenses

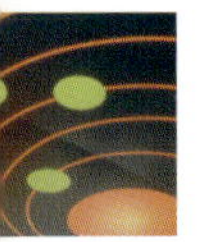

# KODE

Sunrise Village Shopping Center,
Citrus Heights, Calif.

*Studio O+A, San Francisco*

KODE is the flagship retail store for a cellular phone service company marketing to teens.

Research showed that the best demographics in Northern California for opening a teen-focused cellular phone pilot store were in Sacramento. But the research also showed that area teens wanted to shed their suburban identities for more urban ones.

For the space it ended up with, next to a Subway sandwich shop in a strip mall, the retailer wanted a spare and industrial "hangout" feel for teens and with lots of parking. So Studio O+A (San Francisco) stripped the space bare, painted the mechanical equipment and ceiling joists black and put up white walls. A new product by Lonseal gave the floor a polished concrete look. Special flower-shaped product display stands were designed. The designers also developed a display system behind the sales desk with a grid of clear plastic pillows featuring "must-have" phone toys.

Oversized upholstered seating engulfs the shopper, and translucent circular booths create more intimacy.

A local graffiti artist was commissioned to paint one of the walls, and on Friday evenings DJs train kids in the art of spinning records and play music for dancing.

Frosted windows complete the "club" feel, keeping the adult suburban world outside.

**CLIENT**
KODE Mobile, Citrus Heights, Calif. – Victor Frieburg, owner

**DESIGN**
Studio O+A – Primo Orpilla, president; Verda Alexander, principal; Kris Orpilla, Kurin Tu, designers; Linda Sullivan, job captain

**ARCHITECT**
Clem Soga, San Francisco

**OUTSIDE DESIGN CONSULTANT**
ADD Marketing, Los Angeles

**GENERAL CONTRACTOR**
Robert Schmitz, Citrus Heights, Calif.

**SUPPLIERS**
Maharam, Toronto (fabrics); P&K Tool, Hayward, Calif. (fixturing); Lonseal, Carson, Calif. (flooring); Lushlife, Los Angeles, Cortet Studio, Signal Hill, Calif. (furniture); ADD Marketing, Los Angeles (graphics); Halogens, Millbrae, Calif. (lighting); Abet Laminati, Englewood, N.J., Wilsonart Intl., Temple, Texas (laminates); DTank, Los Angeles (props/decoratives); ME Productions, Santa Cruz, Calif. (signage and wallcoverings)

**PHOTOGRAPHY**
David Wakely, San Francisco

PERSONALKODE

Kode
PEEPS

# mishmash

Woodfield Shopping Center, Schaumburg, Ill.

*TOO Inc., Columbus, Ohio*

mishmash, TOO Inc.'s first prototype after being separated from long-time parent company Limited Brands, was designed to be a fun destination for teenage female shoppers.

So the design team introduced such casual "fun" details as decorative retro light fixtures with splashes of orange; 1960s-inspired op art wallcoverings; and a high-quality sound system thumping with current popular music to greet the teen as she enters and accompany her as she shops.

Keeping a relatively small rectangular space flexible, fresh, dynamic and appealing to the targeted customer was only part of the objective. The merchandise also needed to be inviting, easy to find, clearly presented and fun to shop.

The storefront, representing the simplicity of design, is asymmetrical to contrast mishmash with adjacent retailers. A photo mural in the entry identifies the mishmash customer. The display window is framed in light blue translucent vinyl to feature a variety of small items that might otherwise be lost in the typical expansive glass storefront.

With the entry set back at an angle, featured merchandise can be made more inviting by pulling it forward to the leaseline. The mishmash logo is cantilevered over the entry, where it is easy to identify and read.

Architectural planes were suspended down to a residential level. White gypsum board ceilings help break up the perimeter walls by defining featured areas to present lifestyle, cosmetics and accessories. A neutral white palette is balanced by soft hues of blue and green.

**DESIGN**
TOO Inc., Columbus, Ohio – Michael Rayden, president/ceo; Doug Tilson, vp, real estate/store planning; Jackie Francis, director, store planning

**ARCHITECT**
Shremshock Architects Inc., Columbus, Ohio

**GENERAL CONTRACTOR**
Capitol Construction Group, Chicago

**SUPPLIERS**
Muzak, Fort Mill, S.C. (audio); StoreKraft, Beatrice, Nev., OSF, Toronto, IDX, Toronto, Ledan, New York (fixturing); Mohawk Carpet, Dalton, Ga., Hamilton Parker, Columbus, Ohio (flooring); Galerkin Design, Gardena, Calif. (furniture); P+R Group, Chicago (graphics and wallcoverings); Loeb Electric, Columbus, Ohio, Translite Sonoma, Sonoma, Calif. (lighting); Ruggles Sign Co., Versailles, Ky. (signage)

**PHOTOGRAPHY**
Scott Heidelberg, Columbus, Ohio

EXIT
mish mash

## Flexivity

Parkway Plaza Mall, El Cajon, Calif.

*Braga Oris Associates, New York;*
*Upshot, Chicago*

The idea behind Ford Motor Co.'s new, 5500-square-foot concept store is that a car is more than just a means of transportation: it's a medium of expression.

Design firms Braga Oris (New York) and Upshot (Chicago) scripted the store's layout, which includes 16 computer modules where Ford vehicles can be customized virtually, as well as CD-burning stations, audio equipment rooms and a range of automotive accessories. An industrial look is achieved with stainless-steel panels inset into marbleized linoleum flooring. Unbleached canvas drapery hangs in front of the glass and aluminum walls. Orange and white make up the store's high-contrast palette, while large graphic panels communicate Flexivity's central message: "See, hear, alter, create, make it your own."

**CLIENT**
Flexivity, El Cajon, Calif. – Susan Venen-Bock, project manager; Randy Ortiz, executive director, Consumer Connect organization; Greg Scott, marketing manager; Paul Renko, Nicol Birge, associates

**DESIGN**
Braga Oris Associates, New York – Julio Braga, principal/design director; Patricia Oris, principal, concept and strategy; Turgut Basdemir, senior designer; Ali Ucer, designer

**IMPLEMENTATION TEAM**
Upshot, Chicago – John Kelley, ceo; Brian Priest, vp; Koren Nelson, senior art director; Stefanie King, Nathan McClain, art directors

**OUTSIDE DESIGN CONSULTANT**
Hybridia Design, Fairfax, Va.

**ARCHITECT**
Shremshock Architects Inc., Columbus, Ohio

**GENERAL CONTRACTOR**
Gordon Mountjoy Associates, Alisa Viejo, Calif.

**SUPPLIERS**
Progressive Audio, Columbus, Ohio (audio/ video); Armstrong, New York (ceilings); Kenney Drapery Associates Inc., Bronx, N.Y., Dazian, Burbank, Calif., Gilford, Jeffersonville, Ind. (fabrics); The Taylor Group, Brampton, Ont., Soundies, Chicago, MTI, Hillsboro, Ore. (fixturing); Forbo Industries, Hazelton, Pa., Design Sales Associates Inc., Bayside, N.Y., Afco-USA, Gaithersberg, Md., On the Surface, Red Bank, N.J. (flooring); Vitra, New York, ICF Group, New York (furniture); The Taylor Group, Brampton, Ont. (graphics); Lightolier, Fall River, Mass., Zumtobel AG, Dornbirn, Austria (lighting); Abet Laminati, Englewood, N.J. (laminates); The Taylor Group, Brampton, Ont., Radiant Concepts, Toronto (signage); Acoustical Surfaces, Chaska, Minn., VenTec Ltd., Chicago (wallcovering)

**PHOTOGRAPHY**
David Joseph, New York
Mark Steele, Columbus, Ohio

see>change>hear>create=own
check

mplete the ride, make it yours.

own

at Volume 5-10

hear

hear the road at Volume 1

hear the road at volume 5-10.

c  plete the ride

te the ride, make it yours.
own
fashion forw
you are color, shape
and form. you se
you never follow th
Volume 5-10.
EMERGENCY
SERVICE KIT
HELP

# World Duty Free

San Ysidro, Calif.

*Grid2 International, New York*

The border crossing between San Ysidro, Calif., and Tijuana, Mexico, is one of the most heavily trafficked in North America. The challenge to Grid2 International (New York) was to create a duty free store that was relevant to the local culture while still expressing the positioning and brand image of World Duty Free.

The architectural shell consisted of a vast barrel-vaulted gallery, with a rotunda at the far end. The open, airy, contemporary version of a local mercado that developed was a nod toward the local culture. So were the ochre-colored ceiling and terra cotta floor. A 100-foot-long mural celebrates the rich heritage of Mexico in the development of trade and commerce in the region.

Gently curving aisles meander across a terra cotta field, helping define the perimeter into individual shops merchandised according to category and brand. Freestanding islands in the center of the space create an anchor for presentation, also adding to the differentiation of the departments.

To convey the sense of the World Duty Free brand, contemporary design elements – blond wood, stainless steel, edge-lit plexiglass and large duratrans graphics panels – provide a strong up-to-date environment.

Sales have grown 11 percent since the redesign.

**CLIENT**
World Duty Free Americas Inc., Glen Burnie, Md.

**DESIGN**
Grid2 International, New York – Martin Roberts, president; Akka Ma, vp, design; Betty Chow, vp, graphics; Steven Derwoed, senior designer/director of projects; Lucinda Wait, designer; Jeffrey Cook, Jen Reinhart, graphics; Robert Cruise, CAD

**ARCHITECT**
Martinez & Cutri Corp., San Ysidro, Calif.

**OUTSIDE DESIGN CONSULTANT**
Lighting Management Inc., New City, N.Y.

**GENERAL CONTRACTOR**
Nielsen Dillingham, San Ysidro, Calif.

**SUPPLIERS**
Sawitz Fixtures, Carlstadt, N.J. (fixtures); PermaGrain, Newtown Square, Pa., Chromatech, Leeds, U.K. (flooring); First Wood and Laminates, Brooklyn, N.Y., VenTec Ltd., Chicago, Pionite, Auburn, Maine, Chemetal, Easthampton, Mass. (laminates)

**PHOTOGRAPHY**
Peter Paige, Upper Saddle River, N.J.

WORLD
DUTY FREE
Save up to 50% on Cigarettes
Ahorre 50% en Cigarros
Ahorre 50% en Licor
LUCKY STRIKE
Winston
GPC

WORLD
DUTY FREE
GUCCI
BVLGARI
Cartier
Cartier
Cartier
liz claiborne

GIN
VODKA
TEQUILA
RUM
Seagram's VO
Crown Royal

Christian Dior

# San Diego Zoo Store

San Diego

*Esherick Homsey Dodge & Davis, Chicago,*
*and Schwartz Architects, New York*

Created in the 70s, the Jungle Bazaar Gift Shop at the exit to the San Diego Zoo had become outdated and outmoded. Hired by the Zoological Society of San Diego to give the store a more up-to-date look were two architectural firms: Esherick Homsey Dodge & Davis (Chicago) and Schwartz Architects (New York).

The result of that collaboration is the re-christened San Diego Zoo Store, which opened last summer after a $1.8 million renovation. The 11,000-square-foot store – which consists of two buildings flanking the exit path – now features an open, airy environment for displaying products from the zoo's 11 merchandising divisions.

The shop's design theme, "Environments," integrates bamboo, grass, tree and flower images with vibrant colors. Dark wood-paneled interiors have been replaced with a new palette of off-white wall surfaces. The shopping area for grownups is a 6700-square-foot pavilion that features a new skylight. Giant scale murals of bamboo and grass animal habitats highlight the smaller, adjoining children's store. The net effect is a fresh, uncluttered arena for displaying and selling merchandise.

**CLIENT**
The Zoological Society of San Diego – Marge Sheldon, director of merchandising; Steve Fobes, project architect

**DESIGN**
EHDD Architecture, Chicago – Marc L'Italien, project director, project designer; Tomislav Pejic, Rick Feldman, project architects; Marj Brownstein, project manager; Ursula Currie, construction administration; Dylan Jhirad, graphic design; Schwartz Architects, New York – Fred Schwartz, principal; Henry Rollman, project architect

**OUTSIDE DESIGN CONSULTANTS**
Gallegos Lighting Design, Oakland, Calif.; Rutherford & Chekene, Oakland, Calif.; Guttman & Blaevoet, San Francisco; O'Mahoney & Myer, San Francisco; Oppenheim Lewis Inc., San Francisco

**GENERAL CONTRACTOR**
Melhorn Construction, San Diego

**SUPPLIERS**
G.A. Rogers Enterprises, San Diego (vent wood); Millrock Inc., Sanford, Maine (birch plywood); Star Tile Inc., Spring Valley, Calif. (handmade tile); Kead's Hardwood Floors, San Diego (flooring); Landscape Forms Inc., Kalamazoo, Mich. (wood bench); Rembrandt Graphics Inc., Anaheim, Calif. (3M photographic murals); Gary Cornell Painting, San Diego (wallcoverings)

**PHOTOGRAPHY**
Doug Snower Photography, Chicago

f the little thing that
beautiful for

KidStoreKidStoreKidStore

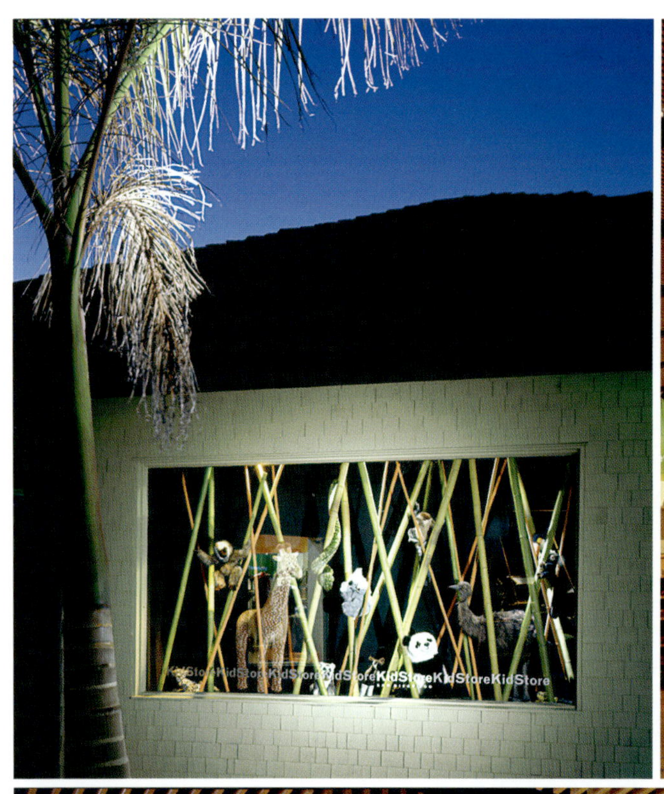

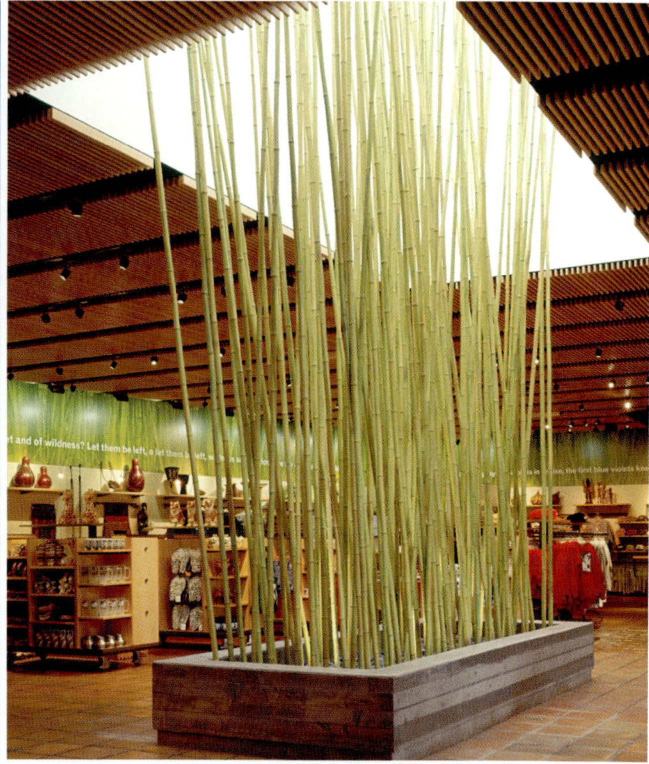

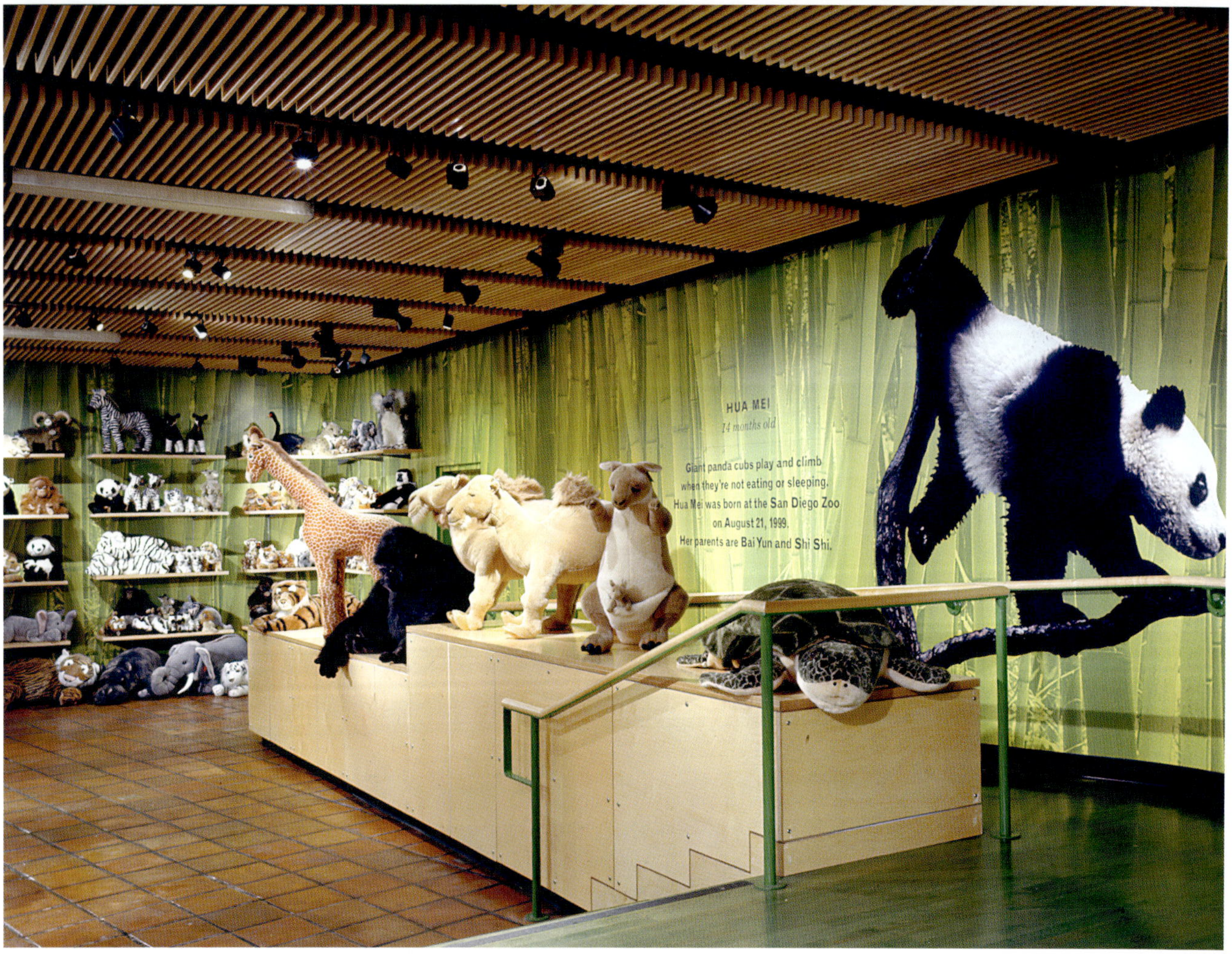
HUA MEI
14 months old
Giant panda cubs play and climb
when they're not eating or sleeping.
Hua Mei was born at the San Diego Zoo
on August 21, 1999.
Her parents are Bai Yun and Shi Shi.

# Bass Pro Shops Outdoor World

Discover Mills, Lawrenceville, Ga.

*Bass Pro Shops Inc. Architects, Springfield, Mo.*

Bass Pro Shops Outdoor World bills itself as the world's leading supplier of premium products for hunting, fishing, camping and boating enthusiasts. Consequently, its stores are designed to bring the great outdoors indoors.

To help realize this vision at its outlet in the new Discover Mills in suburban Atlanta, the company's in-house design firm installed such features as a 30,000-gallon aquarium stocked with fish for casting demonstrations, an indoor archery range and a 43-foot-high climbing wall. These features are meant to enhance customers' visual experiences, provide them with educational information and promote product lines by offering visitors a hands-on chance to try them.

An array of interior structures and custom-designed, artisan-produced elements are strategically placed throughout the store, providing numerous destinations, creating a sense of discovery and drawing customers through the space. Custom-designed chandeliers, adorned with hand-painted acrylic domes, add dimensions of interest and historical context. Bass Pro officials believe the excitement of the environment they've created lies in its ability to make the customer become a part of it and connect with this country's hunting and fishing traditions.

**CLIENT**
Bass Pro Shops, Springfield, Mo. – Tom Jowett, vp, design and development; Tom Gammon, director, construction; Mark Tuttle, director, architecture; Jack Urbec, project manager; Jeff Masters, senior designer; Kelli Bays, interior project manager; Russ Halley, project interior color and materials; Ray Fitzgerald, director, retail planning; Will Clark, marine; Steve Kuhn, loss prevention

**OUTSIDE DESIGN CONSULTANTS**
Butler Rosenbury & Partners, Springfield, Mo.; Spaid Associates, St. Louis; Visualizations LLC, Brookline, Mo.

**GENERAL CONTRACTOR**
Centex Rooney Construction Co. Inc., Plantation, Fla.

**SUPPLIERS**
Design 101, Santa Fe, N.M. (murals); Dream Themes, Tampa, Fla. (arcade targets); Garage Graphics, Springfield, Mo. (signage); Gordon's Fabrications, Springfield, Mo. (log work); Oklahoma Fixture Co., Tulsa, Okla., Lozier, St. Peters, Mo. (fixtures); Sensormatic Electronics Corp., Boca Raton, Fla. (CCTV and EAS systems)

**PHOTOGRAPHY**
Douglas Hill, Atlanta

# Galleria at Roseville kiosk

Roseville, Calif.

*TL Horton Design, Grapeville, Texas*

Urban Retail Properties' Galleria at Roseville in northern California is an elegant mall with an eclectic architectural style – it's adorned with arched ceiling treatments, decorative column capitals and moldings and etched glass. Those features, in turn, are mimicked in the design details of the kiosks that TL Horton Design (Grapeville, Texas) created for this tony retail environment.

To help engender a quality look for the kiosks, Horton used maple veneer and mahogany wood accents. The top of the units features a white soffit with recessed lighting and custom-made column capitals, while the radius top consists of heat-bent frosted acrylic that's back-illuminated with neon.

Identification signage atop the stands mirrors a graphics pattern used throughout the center and in its marketing materials. The kiosks can be used by a variety of retailers, including cellular phone providers and sellers of CD cases.

**CLIENT**
Urban Retail Properties, San Francisco

**DESIGN**
TL Horton Design, Grapevine, Texas – George Garces, president; Stan Zalenski, senior vp; Tony Horton, designer

**PHOTOGRAPHY**
Joe Aker, Houston

GALLERIA AT
ROSEVILLE
Pacific Bell PCS Store
NOKIA
NOKIA
NOKIA
Bath & Body Works
PAGE
CALIFORNIA
Pacific Bell PCS Store

# Reto and the machine

Toronto

*Perennial Inc., Toronto*

Haute cuisine and fast-food are typically worlds apart. Attempting to bridge that chasm is Reto and the machine, a food-court fusion of a revolutionary machine that cooks al dente pasta in 90 seconds and the exotic sauces of world-renowned chef Reto Mathis. Working with those basic ingredients, design firm Perennial Inc. (Toronto) whipped up a 1000-square-foot space on Commerce Court in Toronto in which the Reto brand is reinforced throughout every element of the design and layout.

The food-preparation area is a self-contained unit that serves as a "theater" where chefs entertain customers with their culinary activities. The proprietary pasta machines, coupled with induction units, woks and stainless-steel accents, give the space a clean and modern appearance. The menu board features vivid food images designed to stimulate the appetites of patrons.

Contemporary finishes underscore applied wall graphics that detail the story of Reto, describe the sauces and take readers on a journey of the senses. As a final touch, fresh garnishes are displayed prominently to allow customers to customize their dishes. The result is "extraordinary pasta, fresh and fast," served up in a stimulating setting.

**CLIENT**
Reto Canada, Toronto

**DESIGN**
Perennial Inc., Toronto – Chris Lund, president; Tracy Collett Parkin, manager; Cam Whitworth, Steven Comisso, David Evans, designers; Jill Flaherty, Kirstie Jarvis, Jeff MacGregor, project managers; Sharon Snider, Lisa Kelleher, David Particelli, graphics

**GENERAL CONTRACTOR**
Structure Corp., Toronto

**SUPPLIERS**
Triden Distribution Ltd., Scarborough, Ont. (bench upholstery); Atelier RCM Inc., St. Isidore, Beauce Novol, Que. (fixturing); Stonetile, Toronto (flooring); Kiosk, Toronto (furniture); Octopus Products, Toronto, Wilsonart Intl., Temple, Texas (laminates)

**PHOTOGRAPHY**
Richard Johnson, Toronto

RETO
and the machine
extraordinary
pasta
fresh & fast
Share
our
passion
for pasta.

# Rain

Mercer Street, Toronto

*II BY IV Design Associates, Toronto*

Toronto has become a mecca for Hollywood movie-making, and so the restaurateurs running Rain wanted a chic and sophisticated watering hole, ultra-cool and sensually inviting. This created a special challenge, since the space had previously been a women's prison.

Deflected and reflected light are the key elements of the design by II BY IV Design Associates (Toronto). A wet glow suffuses the entire space, expressed in the internally lit white glass monoliths serving as telephone table and host station, in the service and feature bars, in the transparent vinyl upholstery, in the waterfall-edged white acrylic cocktail tables and in the clear glass drink rail invisibly suspended above discreet footlights along the white-painted brick wall.

Two 10-foot chandeliers of individually suspended light bulbs hover over the crush space just inside the entry, which is centered on a 50-foot wall faced with lacquered pebbles in a mortar bed and fronted by two full-height cascades falling into beds of river rock. A third waterfall trickles among the glass shelves on the theatrically-lit backbar.

The remaining space, subdivided into eating and drinking lounges, uses glass screens and walls of bamboo forests for separation. Areas are further demarcated by top-lit stretched white plastic canopies overhead.

A 10-foot circular lounge, long benches and fully upholstered armless, low-back pull-up units encourage languid sprawling. Harrison Ford and Danny DeVito have already been seen languidly sprawling there.

CLIENT
Rain, Toronto

DESIGN
II BY IV Design Associates Inc., Toronto – Keith Rushbrook, Dan Menchions, Jenny Lee, designers

OUTSIDE DESIGN CONSULTANTS
ICI Construction Ltd., Toronto; ESTI Consultants, Toronto; Atkins Van Groll Engineering, Thornhill, Ont.; HGC Engineering, Toronto

GENERAL CONTRACTOR
ICI Construction Ltd., Toronto

SUPPLIERS
Kiosk, Toronto (bar stools); Louis Interiors, Toronto (furniture); Stretch Ceiling Barrisol, Toronto (ceiling feature); Matrix Metal, Toronto (metalwork); Vast Interiors Custom Glass & Mirror, Concord, Ont. (glazing); studio b, Toronto (bubble chairs); Vimax Consultants, Toronto (slatemax walls for water feature); Alpha and Omega, Mississauga, Ont. (structural steel); Granolite Co. Ltd., Toronto (pebble walls); Maharam, Toronto (fabric); Italinteriors, Toronto (dining stools); ISA Intl. Inc., Toronto (custom dining tables); House of Bamboo, Toronto (bamboo); European Hotel and Restaurant, Mississauga, Ont. (kitchen equipment); ma zone home decor, Toronto (accessories); Rafael Painting, Toronto (painting); Stalree Cabinets & Millwork, Toronto (custom millwork); Litemore/Eurolite, Toronto (lighting fixtures)

PHOTOGRAPHY
David Whittaker, Toronto

rain

# L.C.B.O.
# Vintages Wine Store

ManuLife Centre, Toronto

*Watt IDG, Toronto*

The Liquor Control Board of Ontario wanted a wine store that would brand its more-specialized vintage selections. The objective, however, was not to create a store that was overtly upscale, but rather an approachable urban mini-store with a comfortable atmosphere.

Watt IDG (Toronto) created a combination of crisp architectural and fixture details married to a blend of subtle colors and textures. The clean layout was to control traffic effectively.

A glass storefront exposes the entire store to the mall concourse. A simple identity wall both grounds the brand and announces the arrival of the retailer's catalog (a must-read of cachet for die-hard connoisseurs).

The window display consists of crate-like pedestals that highlight monthly features and open floor fixtures that organize vintages into bins (while also helping to maintain back-up stock on the sales floor).

Modulated fixtures are designed to accept full or half cases of product. Cubed wall fixtures divide vintages into bin-like compartments. Floor fixtures are designed to display vintages in formal horizontal positions. Gondola ends display mass quantities of promotional product, and are equipped with chalkboards for impromptu p-o-p information.

A wine cabinet is filled with rare and expensive vintages. The locked unit is both humidity- and temperature-controlled.

**CLIENT**
Liquor Control Board of Ontario, Toronto – Jackie Bonic, director; Michelle Griffin, design manager; Janet Glover, graphics

**DESIGN**
Watt IDG, Toronto – Ron Harris, managing director, creative and operations; David Newman, creative director; Ron Mazereeuw, senior designer

**GENERAL CONTRACTOR**
Rutherford Contracting, Gormley, Ont.

**SUPPLIERS**
Hutton Bielman, London, Ont. (fixturing); Karndean, Toronto (flooring); Juno Lighting, Toronto (lighting)

**PHOTOGRAPHY**
Richard Johnson, Toronto

VINTAGES
ROSÉ 1999
$15.75
VINTAGES
ORGANIC

# freshgo

Potomac Woods Plaza, Rockville, Md.

*Grid2 International, New York*

When Giant Foods Inc. (Landover, Md.) sought to create a specialty supermarket that would appeal to time-starved customers looking for healthy, fresh and convenient meal solutions, it turned to Grid2. The resulting 17,000-square-foot prototype, decorated in bright greens and orange and interspersed with oversized icons of eating utensils, is part café, part drug store and part take-away dining.

At the entrance, a branded Volkswagen Beetle is parked, signaling to shoppers that freshgo is something unique and exciting. Inside, departments are differentiated by changes in flooring and ceiling treatments, along with large signage and murals. Unlike typical grocery stores, staple items like milk are placed in the front of the store instead of the back, facilitating a quick, simple shopping process. This easygoing layout lends itself to the concept's tagline, "How you freshgo is up to you."

**CLIENT**
Giant Foods Inc., Landover, Md. – David Zwartendijk, director, new ventures

**DESIGN**
Grid2 International, New York – Martin Roberts, president; Akka Ma, principal-in-charge; Betty Chow, principal, graphics; Steven Derwoed, project designer; Brian Hack, project manager; Jennifer Reinhart and Jeffrey Cook, graphic designers; Maggie Perczek and Marek Kusio, designers; Robert Cruse, CAD

**OUTSIDE DESIGN CONSULTANT**
Lighting Management Inc., New City, N.Y.

**SUPPLIERS**
Interfinish, Chicago (ceilings); Armstrong World Industries, Lancaster, Pa., Baldwin Harbor, New York, Amtico Intl., Atlanta (flooring); Amerlux, Fairfield, N.J. (lighting); Impressions, Lorton, Va. (signage and graphics)

**PHOTOGRAPHY**
Peter Paige, Upper Saddle River, N.J.

# Sunoco A Plus

Gap Newport Pike, Avondale, Pa.

*Miller Zell, Atlanta*

The objective was to create a marketplace-focused convenience store format for under $120 a square foot.

The positioning and marketing strategies were to provide quality food products, while still meeting the convenience needs of the existing Sunoco customer, and to broaden the customer base beyond Joe Six-Pack to the soccer mom.

Miller Zell (Atlanta) developed a unique "inside-out" design approach, based on the ideal positioning of key merchandise categories. It created both physical and visual separations between the traditional convenience products and the new food-service offerings, both proprietary and co-branded.

A customer decompression zone at the entry is followed by a "power promotion" zone just one step beyond. The existing structure allowed for a 26-foot ceiling height, giving a strong marketplace feel to the entire store. Each of the prime categories is distinguished with its own façade. The exterior conveys a sense of tradition/marketplace. And through the use of curved canopy and clear glass, there's a strong sense of openness between forecourt and backcourt. The category "storefronts" have product towers built in to improve the cross-sell of additional products within the category.

The ability to standardize the design elements in a space-adaptable package reduced construction costs for the store and car wash by 11 percent. Sunoco has utilized the design in three different size formats, from 720 to 1200 to 2400 square feet.

**CLIENT**

Sunoco, Philadelphia – Chris Butron, Gary Bromley, Wayne Hicks, Mark Borosky

**DESIGN**

Miller Zell, Atlanta – Ian Rattray, David Kotke, Tod Lawrence, Tom Ertler, Jim Matthews, Wendy Weiner, Lis Diaz, Ann Otterness, Bob Degroff, Sandy Miller, designers

**ARCHITECT**

Lester M. Stein, Bethlehem, Pa.

**OUTSIDE DESIGN CONSULTANTS**

Antista Fairclough, Atlanta; Lighting Management, New City, N.Y.

**GENERAL CONTRACTOR**

Bohler Engineering, N. Wales, Pa.

**SUPPLIERS**

Wilsonart Intl., Temple, Texas (laminates); Hubbell, Christiansburg, Va. (lighting); Armstrong World Industries, Lancaster, Pa. (ceiling)

**PHOTOGRAPHY**

John Grunke, Atlanta

Gulliver's
COFFEE COMPANY
Krispy Kreme
DOUGHNUTS

# Famous Players Starcite

Olympic Park, Montreal

*Watt IDG, Toronto*

How to give a movie theater complex significant destination appeal in the now-desolate, about-to-be-rejuvenated Olympic Park in a remote Montreal neighborhood? The solution was to make the theater a show in itself.

The entertainment begins even before the movie does. By animating the usually static architectural and design elements, the show that Watt IDG (Toronto) created integrates the external and internal experiences with a color-morphing light show that bathes the exterior of the building.

Patrons are greeted by an open-concept box office, a large LED display and a poster-box screen that shrouds an interactive game facility. Overscaled patterns and forms and bold signage create a larger-than-life concept. Highly durable materials – linoleum floors, metal and sparkling laminates – endure the high traffic and accompanying abuse.

A dynamic ceiling treatment of discs, neon rings and large sound domes mimic the interactive games that fill the lobby's entrance.

An interior light show sits atop the central popcorn island. Colored and patterned light is projected onto the stretched fabric discs above and onto the glazed lobby wall. Sandblasted images of film stars catch the animating light and color. Varying levels of daylight and varied-light programs from DMX help establish different moods throughout the day – a dynamic, chameleon-like space that is always evolving.

**CLIENT**
Famous Players, a Viacom company, Toronto – John Bailey, coo; Ron Rivet, executive director, design and construction

**DESIGN**
Watt IDG, Toronto – Ron Harris, managing director, creative and operations; Andrew Gallici, creative director; Donna Lawson, co-creative director; Paulis Ciskevicius, senior designer; John MacDonald, Tad Gracz, James Janz, designers

**ARCHITECT**
Ruccolo and Faubert Architects, Montreal

**OUTSIDE DESIGN CONSULTANTS**
Stephen Pollard, lighting designer, Toronto; Commarts, Boulder, Colo., (event designers)

**GENERAL CONTRACTOR**
Divco Ltd., Montreal

**SUPPLIERS**
Data Display, Ronkonkoma, N.Y. (audio/video); Alaska Millwork, Ottawa, Ont. (fixturing); Forbo Marmoleum, Toronto (flooring); ULA Intl., Toronto (furniture); Trans-Formes L.M. Inc., Montreal (props/decoratives)

**PHOTOGRAPHY**
Richard Johnson, Toronto

SURF CITY
Wetzel's Pretzels
MIKES
BEN & JERRY'S
CINÉMAS
6
7
8
9
10
11
14
15
16
17

# Rave Motion Pictures

Hickory Creek, Texas

*dsgn associates, Dallas*

The project was immense: a 57,000-square-foot, 108-seat cinema with 16 stadium auditoriums, three concession areas, an arcade, regional offices and parking. The 9.9-acre site lies adjacent to a suburban retail center, sits along a major roadway and is near a low-density suburban residential area.

The building addresses the need to create a statement along the broad sweep of the freeway by splitting the normally rectangular box into two wings and rotating each wing around the middle, thus providing a viewing axis to both north- and south-bound traffic.

This also creates an entry courtyard on the exterior, which acts as a buffer between the parking lot and the lobby. And it results in shorter travel distances to the auditoriums.

Layering of opaque, translucent and transparent materials reinforces the vocabulary of the design. Light filters into the lobby, courtyard and media tower through tinted glass, clear glass and aluminum screens. The layering is carried through into the lobby, secondary lobbies, auditoriums and restrooms by a video collage and other print media. These graphic devices appear above translucent plastic ceilings, behind the opaque concessions and ticket box graphics panels, previewed on plasma screens and video monitors, even embedded in logos in the limestone floor.

The design process included the concept name, corporate logo and custom signage.

**CLIENT**
Rave Motion Pictures, Dallas

**DESIGN**
dsgn associates, Dallas – Cal Young, design principal; Jett Buler, Monica Miranda, Mary Beth Clark, Tommy Tenery, Jamie Crawley, Peter Snyder, Nancy Weeks, designers

**OUTSIDE DESIGN CONSULTANT**
Dimensional Innovations, Overland Park, Kan.

**GENERAL CONTRACTOR**
Saad & Cooke, Mobile, Ala.

**SUPPLIERS**
Wilsonart Intl., Temple, Texas, Formica Corp., Cincinnati, Pionite, Auburn, Maine, Abet Laminati, Englewood, N.J. (laminates); Atlas Carpet, Los Angeles (flooring); Armstrong World Industries, Lancaster, Pa. (ceiling)

**PHOTOGRAPHY**
Mark Olsen, Dallas

pure
fresh
taste
DASANI
[R
10 HULK
11 FINDINGNEM
12 FINDINGNEM
13 RUGRATGOW
14 BRUCEALMIG
15 DUMB&DUMB
16 HULK
17 HULK
18 2FAST2FUR
RAVE THE

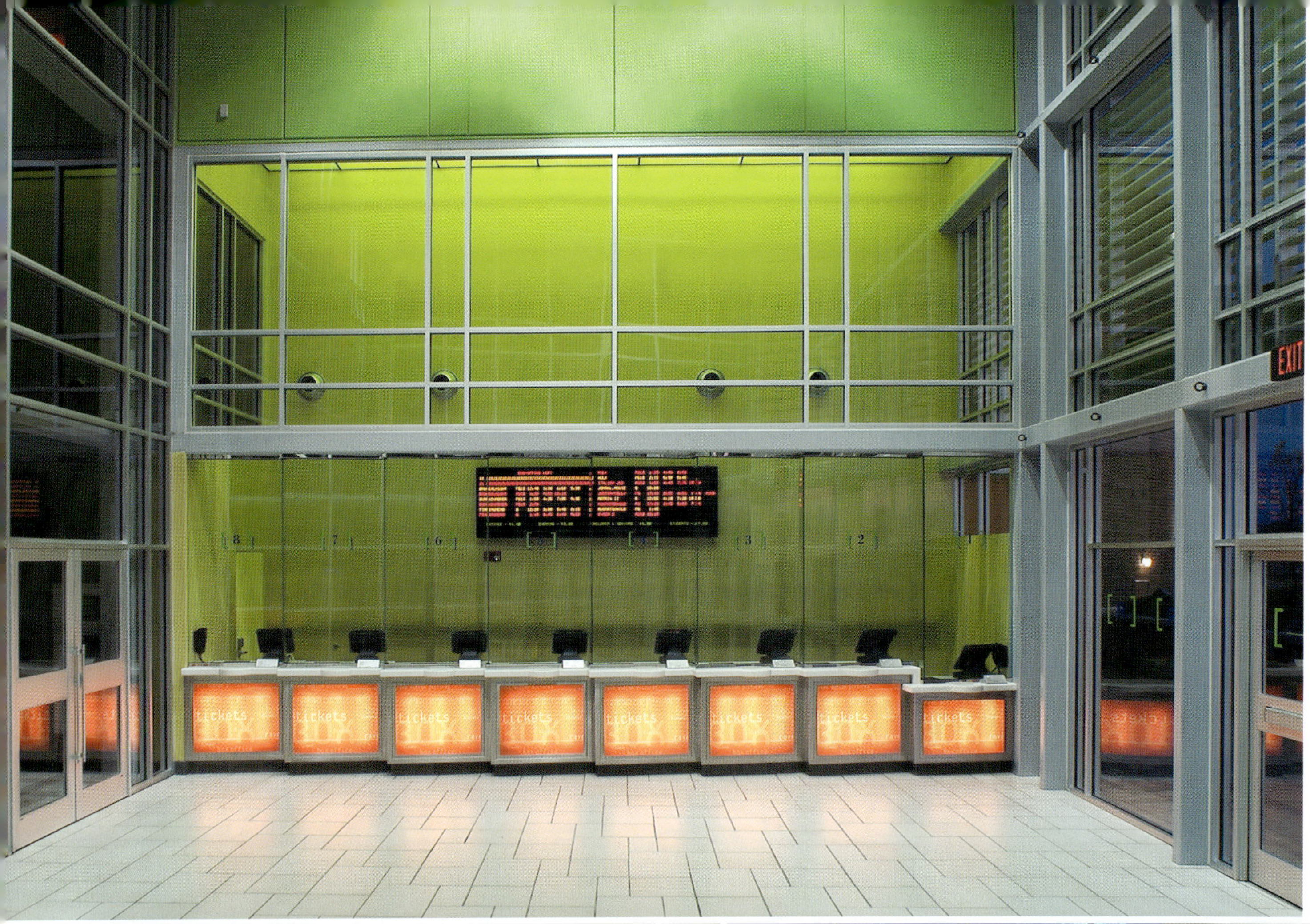
EXIT
tickets

candy
popcorn

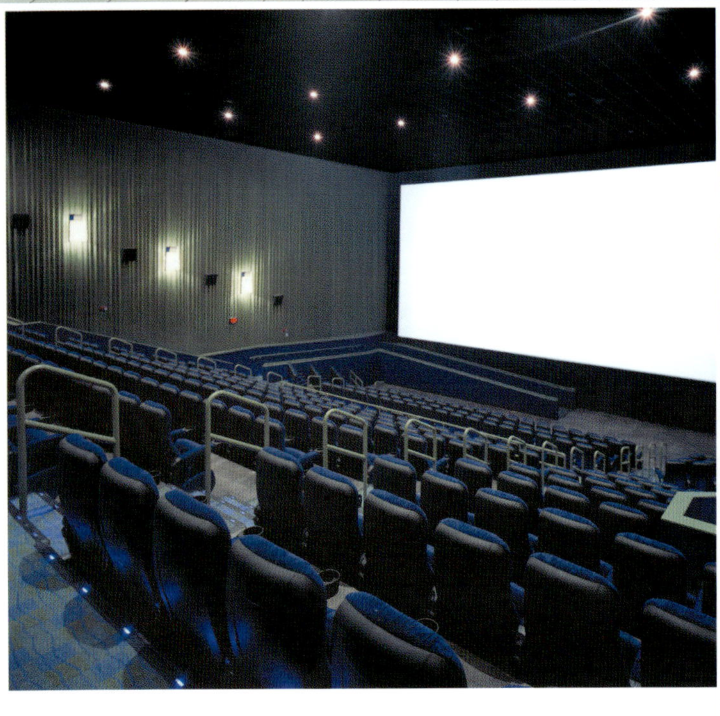

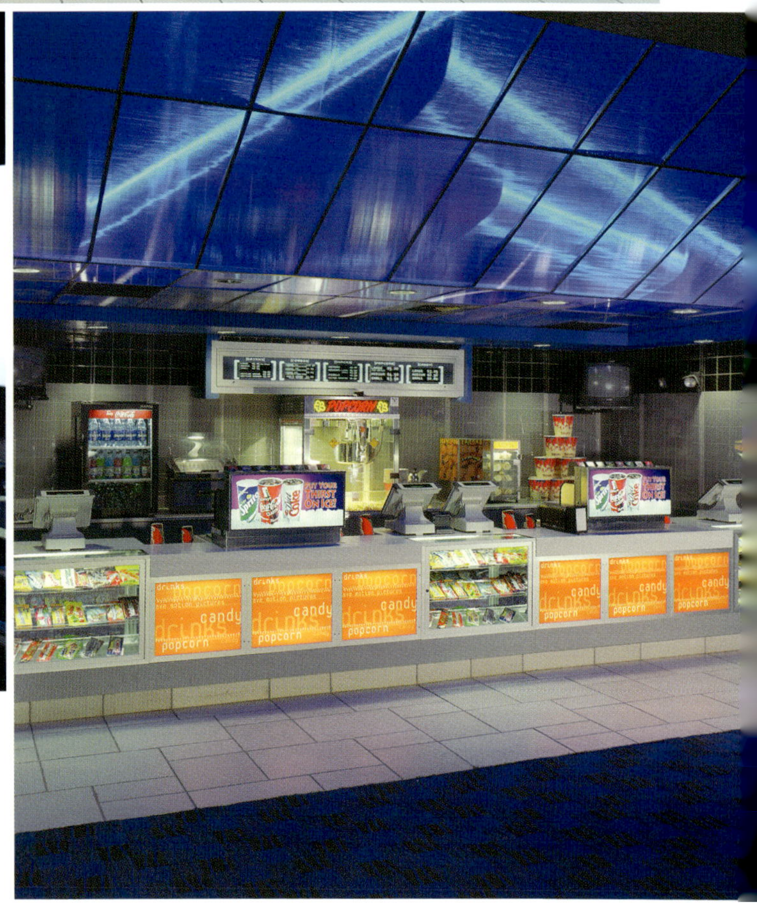

# embarq

Markville Shopping Centre, Markham, Ont.

*Fiorino Design Inc., Toronto*

Designed to occupy kids and bored spouses in the mall setting, embarq lounges convey relaxation, stimulation and security. embarq kids, executed with stimulating teal and yellow colors, contains toddler and preschool activities in an enclosed area. Options for older kids exist in an open arrangement immediately outside, featuring an aquarium, bug farm and reading and science areas.

The adjacent adult lounge is meant to be a calm oasis, complete with café seating, newspapers and magazines, complimentary gourmet coffee, waterfalls, a fireplace, CD-listening stations and laptop computers. Taupe and green tones create a more muted palette.

**CLIENT**
Cadillac Fairview Corp., Toronto – Susan Williams, director, market research; Fran Moore, associate

**DESIGN**
Fiorino Design Inc., Toronto – Nella Fiorino, principal; Vilija Gacionis, Amor Jalandoon, Vasco Pires, Mike Wilson, designers

**OUTSIDE DESIGN CONSULTANT**
Engage Communications, Toronto

**GENERAL CONTRACTOR**
Structural Corp., Toronto

**SUPPLIERS**
Entertainment Technology, Toronto (audio/ visual); Tandem Fabrics Inc., Cambridge, Ont., Maharam, Toronto (fabrics); Atelier RCM Inc., St. Isidore, Beauce Novol, Que. (fixturing); Forbo Industries, Concord, Ont., Floorworks Intl., Toronto (flooring); Kiosk Furniture, Toronto (furniture); Eurolite, Toronto (lighting); Nevamar, Odenton, Md., Laminart, Mississauga, Ont. (laminates); Benjamin Moore, Toronto, Sico Paints, Etobicoke, Ont. (paint)

**PHOTOGRAPHY**
David Whittaker, Toronto

# Häfele Showroom

New York

*STUDIOS Architecture, New York*

Häfele, the international, Germany-based architectural hardware manufacturer and supplier, wanted much more out of its New York showroom than simply a place to display products. It wanted a multi-activity center that would serve as a resource for the architectural, design and building communities, with informal meeting and lounge areas and seminar, conference and lecture capabilities. And it wanted a celebration of hardware, in form and in function.

The space also needed to be flexible, to accommodate both large-scale events and day-to-day business needs.

STUDIOS Architecture (New York) rearranged mechanical systems in the 5100-square-foot space to create a layout that would do justice to the full-height storefront windows and an open ceiling of nearly 14 feet. Hung perforated metal ceiling screens in each column bay unify the space. The sales office was placed on a raised platform in the back to give the staff some privacy while still being able to see the entire showroom.

Displays – built-ins along the wall, moveable within the space – were designed to show the company's products in both functional and intriguing settings. A lowered, curved soffit creates an intimately scaled area for kitchen displays. More abstract feature displays were placed at the front entrance to catch the eyes of passersby, who are then drawn in by back-lit shelves, drawers and containers.

Other displays are festooned throughout the showroom behind sliding doors, hinged doors, drawers and other moving parts to engage visitors, encouraging them to touch and interact with the displays. The hardware products themselves were placed in settings of maple, glass, stainless steel, polyethylene and poured concrete.

**CLIENT**
Häfele America, New York – Ed Cohen, owner; John Hossli, president; Philip Martin, marketing manager; Karl-Heinz Kraft, Joy Stancevic, store planning

**DESIGN**
STUDIOS Architecture, New York – Todd DeGarmo, principal; Linda Jacobs, project manager; Alethea Cheng, project architect; Stephanie Slack, designer

**GENERAL CONTRACTOR**
Archibuild Construction Management, New York

**SUPPLIERS**
Erik Cabinets, Hamilton, Ont. (millwork, fixtures); Heritage, St. Charles, N.Y. (kitchens); Long Island Concrete, Centereach, N.Y. (flooring); Joel Berman Glass, Vancouver (cast glass); Bedlam Brass, Garfield, N.J. (ceiling screens); Abet Laminati, Englewood, N.J. (laminates); Tech Lighting, Skokie, Ill. (lighting)

**PHOTOGRAPHY**
Andrew Bordwin, New York

## Fred Lavery Co.

Birmingham, Mich.

*JGA Inc., Southfield, Mich.*

Designing a showroom for Porsche, Land Rover and Audi that allows the dealer's brand to shine without getting overwhelmed by the car brands is a considerable challenge.

Through a creative collaboration of architecture and design, designers from JGA (Southfield, Mich.) created a luxury showcase of automotive design. The architectural challenge was to integrate three luxury automotive brands into one dealer showcase. The result is a sleek, textural showroom with curvilinear lines that brings the upscale brands together under the signature Fred Lavery umbrella.

By using the porcelain tile floor as the canvas for the vehicles, brands are defined by distinctive shapes. For example, Audi vehicles are exhibited on the brand's iconic rings, Land Rovers on circles echoing its trademark and Porsches on squares between the other two brands.

Expansive glass exposure on a major local thoroughfare creates an illuminated billboard for passing traffic. Sales offices are defined by sweeping, scalloped, frosted glass partitions and clear, curvilinear glass panels. The customer waiting area features Le Corbusier club chairs and Eileen Gray glass and chrome steel tube tables. Even the restrooms are finished with high-polished surfaces and a blue neon art accent.

**CLIENT**
Fred Lavery Co., Birmingham, Mich. – Fred Lavery, president; Joyce Raymond, project manager

**DESIGN**
JGA Inc., Southfield, Mich. – Tony Camilletti, senior vp; Mike Curtis, creative director; Stephanie Bourdon, design manager, color and materials

**ARCHITECT**
Lukenbach Ziegelman Architects PLLC, Birmingham, Mich.

**GENERAL CONTRACTOR**
Midwest Commercial Services, Pontiac, Mich.

**SUPPLIERS**
Virginia Tile, Farmington Hills, Mich. (flooring); Stone Designs, Glendale Heights, Ill. (granite); Bolyu Contract, Adairsville, Ga. (carpet); Stone Panels, Carrollton, Texas (architectural wall panel); Surface Materials, Solon, Ohio (paint); Reid Glass Co., Southfield, Mich. (glass); Engineered Environments, Toronto (ceiling); Illuminart, Ypsilanti, Mich. (lighting); Ford & Earl, Troy, Mich. (sign/graphics); Facility Matrix, Pontiac, Mich., Gordon Intl., New York, Design Within Reach, San Francisco, Hampton Products, Pontiac, Mich. (furniture)

**PHOTOGRAPHY**
Laszlo Regos Photography, Berkley, Mich.

# Speedo

London

*Checkland Kindleysides, Leicester, England*

Speedo International (London) wanted its first corporate-owned store to reflect the full-spectrum of the brand's journey. The 2700-square-foot, two-level flagship on Neal Street in London's Covent Garden doesn't just plumb the depths of its performance swimwear. It runs ashore with the fun-loving beach clothes of Speedo's Australian homeland.

"In the U.K. and the U.S., the Speedo brand is known for its sports affiliation," explains Clive Hunt, senior designer at Checkland Kindleysides (Leicester, England), the firm that handled the store design. "We wanted to create a global flagship that returned Speedo to its leisure roots in Australia."

Checkland Kindleysides left the space's unique infrastructure mostly undisturbed. But some features, like the storefront, couldn't slip by without a facelift.

The new front, laced with anodized aluminum and lustrous stainless steel, features a frameless glass entry and a large display window. A new, stylized Speedo sign glows above the doorway – an illuminated blue lozenge brandishing the characteristic red boomerang.

At the ground-floor entrance, four acrylic ceiling panels, decorated with melted resin and colored light, create a blue and aqua rippled-water effect – a shimmering contrast to the sunnier white and orange tones of the interior surfaces. The sandy floor tiles have been embossed with a wave pattern, similar to the effect created on the sand when the tide goes out.

At the bottom of the stairs in the basement, a wetsuit stands out against a luminous white mannequin; dark athletic swimsuits adorn the walls, precisely arranged on torso-shaped hangers. Elliptical bench seats, which nest glowing lightboxes in the center of their soft fabric, seem to hover beside the dressing rooms.

The dressing rooms themselves are pertinent nodes of the flagship, with doors resembling portals on a ship. But Hunt is quick to add that the doors' curved shape is "directly related to the merchandising system, to achieve a kind of style synergy around the store." Besides the simulated sound of waves, each high-tech fitting room is also equipped with a call button that illuminates a light on the door and buzzes to alert attendants.

**CLIENT**
Speedo International, London – Georgina Collicutt, international brand manager

**DESIGN**
Checkland Kindleysides, Leicester, England – Wendy Ingham, account director; Karen Robertson and Tony Bell, senior project managers; Lee Draycott and Clive Hunt, senior designers

**SUPPLIERS**
Pel, London (audio/visual); Checkland Kindleysides, London (fixturing, furniture, mannequins, props and graphics); Amtico Intl., Atlanta (flooring); Into Lighting, London (lighting); Sygnet Signs, Leicester, England (signage); Benchline Products, Ossett, England (shopfitting)

**PHOTOGRAPHY**
Adrian Wilson, Macclesfield, England

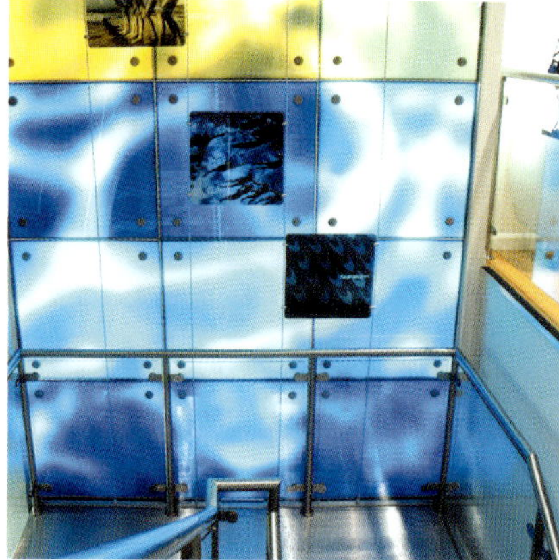

SPEEDO
SPEEDO
SPEEDO
fast skin
SPEEDO fast skin

INDEPENDENTS DAY

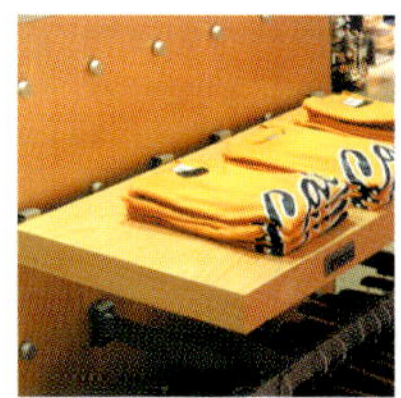

# 5
# STORES AND RETAIL SPACES

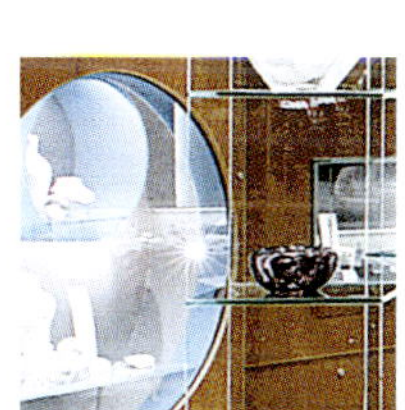

## Fashion Statement

Wyckoff, N.J.

*Kepron Architect, Englewood, N.J.*

Fashion Statement is a small, independent, classic-yet-contemporary specialty apparel store in upscale Wyckoff, N.J. "The typical female Wyckoff resident is a stay-at-home mom in her 40s," says owner Sheryl Brian, "active in her children's school and other activities. She's affluent, college-educated, physically fit and has sophisticated taste in clothing, decorating and dining."

The design objective for Englewood, N.J., architect David Kepron was to create a unique, "classic contemporary" flair, an environment that's bright and clean, and a backdrop for multiple vendors.

Kepron called his design concept "eclectic-chic," contrasting the textural qualities of rich surface materials (crushed velvet, faux finishes and decorative metals) with clean geometries and light steel and wood details.

Large feature walls were created to merchandise goods in front of the windows. Elliptical tables allow for the possibility of bulk-folded presentations and also promote uninterrupted views through the space to the perimeter walls. Existing columns were utilized as vertical merchandisers.

**CLIENT**
Fashion Statement, Wyckoff, N.J. – Sheryl Brian, owner

**DESIGN**
Kepron Architect, Englewood, N.J. – David Kepron, Brian James, Will Tolentino, Lu Kepron

**OUTSIDE DESIGN CONSULTANT**
Glen Gray Construction, Mahwah, N.J. (general contractor)

**SUPPLIERS**
MG Concepts, Central Islip, N.Y., B&N Industries, San Carlos, Calif. (fixtures); Chemetal, Easthampton, Mass. (laminates); sevencontinents, Toronto (mannequins); Barsouv, New York (fabrics)

**PHOTOGRAPHY**
Andrea Brizzi, New York

## UThreads

San Francisco International Airport,
San Francisco

*Tsao Design Group, San Francisco*

Licensed college apparel meets airport retailing in this new concept called UThreads at San Francisco International Airport. California's top universities sought a market for their apparel, gifts and souvenirs in one of America's fastest-growing retail sectors – the travelers between planes, heading for planes or waiting out interminable security delays.

According to Ellen Schumm, principal of Tsao Design Group (San Francisco), "among the design objectives was to create retailing that was not just another T-shirt store. The merchandise is high-quality athletic and sports fashion goods from Russell Athletic and Gear for Sports, plus desk accessories, neckwear, watches and diploma frames."

On a more practical level, Tsao Design had to create a store that was durable ("airport traffic is brutal!"), efficient ("airport stores are small") and economical ("we had a very limited design and construction budget").

"The finishes, fixtures and integrated graphics create a distinctive atmosphere," Schumm says. "Architecture and graphics use a finish and materials palette – natural maple, stained concrete, whites and browns – that complements the typically vibrant collegiate merchandise."

Using standard hardware, the fixtures are adaptable to both hard- and soft-line products. Sliding panels in the perimeter millwork, with storage shelving behind, maximize stock area. And plastic and wood veneer laminates protect the fixture edges from damage due to rolling luggage.

**CLIENT**
UThreads, San Francisco – Maryann Mohn, Fred Piccirilli, owners

**DESIGN**
Tsao Design Group, San Francisco – Ellen Schumm, project principal; Martin Oestlund, project designer; Allyson Kovas, graphic designer

**OUTSIDE DESIGN CONSULTANTS**
P. L. Annuzzi Inc., Burlingame, Calif. (general contractor); S.F. Lighting Design, San Francisco (lighting); Encon, Los Altos, Calif. (mechanical/electrical engineer)

**SUPPLIERS**
Arnold and Egan, San Francisco (fixtures); Construction and Audio Services, San Rafael, Calif. (audio/video); Millennium Display, Hempstead, N.Y., Golden Gate Sign, San Francisco (graphics); Ardex Engineered Cements, Coraopolis, Pa. (stained concrete flooring)

**PHOTOGRAPHY**
Tom Rider, Petaluma, Calif.

COLLEGIATE
THREADS
U
APAREL · GIFTS
STANFORD
UNIVERSITY
EXIT
Cal

Master's Degree
Maples Pavilion
Freedom Blow
Graduation
Cal
STANFORD
UNIVERSITY
CALIFORNIA
Cal
UC BERKELEY

CAL
Cal
UNIVERSITY

UCLA
Bachelor of Arts
Telegraph Avenue
Campus Drive
The Farm
Exams
THE QUAD
Zellerbach
Grad School

# Freyja Collection

Tecumseh Mall, Windsor, Ont.

*Watt IDG, Toronto*

And how would a retailer go about honoring Freyja, the Norwegian goddess of love?

Watt IDG (Toronto) chose to base the new Freyja Collection gift and jewelry store, in the Tecumseh Mall (Windsor, Ont.), on the story of the goddess who "shed tears of gold" and "sprinkled morning dew from her hair."

"Freyja Collection has created a new shopping experience by offering sterling silver, stone jewelry and gifts, and was looking to expand into home- or life-related gifts and specialty items," says Ann Bada Crema, executive director of creative operations at Watt IDG. "Our challenge was to shift an existing retail concept away from the imported handicrafts that made up 80 percent of its mix and toward a sharply focused jewelry-dominant environment."

The representation of wind, water and sand are reflected by the use of color and materials – in particular, natural sand tones and shades of greens and blues.

"This design is based upon the mystical qualities of the circle," says Bada Crema, "a series of circular shapes layered from the planning of the showcases through to the ceilings, walls and architectural elements. Wall displays containing frosted blue concentric circles and horizontal glass shelves enabled two focal points of display.

"The undulating forms of the space and the subtle communication elements within the showcases," she continues, "were intended to comfort customers while engaging them in the merchandise. The simplicity of the design leaves the merchandise as the hero."

**CLIENT**
Freyja Collection, Oldcastle, Ont. – Matte Malec, president

**DESIGN**
Watt IDG, Toronto – Ann Bada Crema, executive director, creative operations; Cheryl Good, designer, graphics; Thom Antonio, managing director, graphics; Colin MacFayden, creative director

**OUTSIDE DESIGN CONSULTANT**
Primary Developments, Oshawa, Ont. (general contractor)

**SUPPLIERS**
Primary Developments, Oshawa, Ont. (fixtures); Sullivan Source, Toronto (flooring); Octopus Products, Toronto (corrugated board); Watt/IDG, Toronto (graphics)

**PHOTOGRAPHY**
Richard Johnson, Interior Images, Toronto

# The Salvador Dali Museum

Salvador Dali Museum Gift Store,
St. Petersburg, Fla.

*Creative Arts Unlimited, Pinellas Park, Fla.*

The Salvador Dali Museum (St. Petersburg, Fla.) wanted to improve the sales performance of its 4000-square-foot bookstore. Creative Arts Unlimited (Pinellas Park, Fla.) was called on to come up with a more productive fixturing and visual merchandising system, but one that reflected the surrealist artist's unique personality and sensibilities.

"We began by creating core fixturing and a focal icon," says Creative Arts president Roger Barganier. "The fixtures would be called upon to present the wide variety of constantly changing custom merchandise. We designed two-way and three-way units and nested table sets. The table sets featured built-in abstract forms to hold T-shirts, beach towels, neckties

and the like. The colors and shapes of these pieces were derived from design elements of Dali's work. Dyed maple and maple veneers were used in the construction of these fixtures, and their additional components were hand-sculpted."

All fixturing was arranged around a 10-foot-tall revolving icon of dyed maple, featuring a blue glowing realization of one of Dali's pieces of imagery. "Our dimensional sculpture glowed with an eerie halo," says Barganier, "thanks to a recessed outline of black lights sandwiched between sheets of ultra violet-sensitive acrylic. A Venus de Milo image was chosen because the museum is famous for housing many of the best examples of the artist's work with this motif."

The shop sells not only the usual array of posters, books and accessories but also a line of Salvador Dali fragrances and cosmetics.

**CLIENT**
Salvador Dali Museum Gift Store, St. Petersburg, Fla.

**DESIGN**
Creative Arts Unlimited, Pinellas Park, Fla. – Roger Barganier, president; Brian Chan, 3-D computer technician; Bruce Merenda, designer, visual merchandising consultant

**SUPPLIER**
Creative Arts Unlimited, Pinellas Park, Fla. (fixtures, props, decoratives)

**PHOTOGRAPHY**
Greg Wilson, Sarasota, Fla.

# Barefoot Books

Cambridge, Mass.

*Monastero & Associates, Cambridge, Mass.*

Barefoot Books (Cambridge, Mass.) publishes colorful, richly illustrated children's books with cross-cultural themes. It had traditionally sold its books (plus CDs, gift cards, wrapping paper and original artwork) through catalogs and over the Internet.

For its first-ever retail store, it asked Cambridge-based Monastero & Associates to "translate the strong brand image into a physical space with flexibility of use," says design principal Nina Monastero.

The firm developed the store's concept around the retailer's mission statement: "Celebrating art and story with books that open the hearts and minds of children from all walks of life, inspiring them to read deeper, search farther and explore their own creative gifts."

So, says Monastero, a small Play Tent in the front of the store, and a larger Story-teller's Tent further inside the store, "contribute to the magical feel and create fun places for children to play while their parents shop." The tents, which are interpretations of sections of the company's web site, are also used for special events – storytelling, puppet shows and arts and crafts workshops.

A wooden post-and-panel fixture system developed by Monastero & Associates is an adjustable way to display products of different sizes. The fixture panels lining the store's perimeter not only form a backdrop for window displays but are also a means of controlling the daylight that streams into the space.

The fixtures, casework, bookcases and tables are painted in vibrant colors and decorated with elements of whimsy. Round display tables are covered with appliqued cloths (created by two of Barefoot Books' artists), creating tactile artwork for children to see and feel. Custom cutout tabletop book-holders use artwork from the book collection to add merchandising height.

**CLIENT**
Barefoot Books, Cambridge, Mass.

**DESIGN**
Monastero & Associates, Cambridge, Mass. – Nina Monastero, AIA, principal; Edie Twining, designer

**OUTSIDE DESIGN CONSULTANT**
Ripman Lighting Design, Belmont, Mass.

**SUPPLIERS**
C.W. Keller & Associates, Plaistow, N.H. (fixtures); Boston Upholstery, W. Roxbury, Mass. (upholstery); Fine Garden Art, Lee, N.H., Sally Dean, Marshfield, Mass. (props/decoratives); SRP Signs, Waltham, Mass. (signage); John Ryan Production Services, Boston (tent installation)

**PHOTOGRAPHY**
Lucy Chen, Somerville, Mass.

Early Learning

# Ybor City Museum

Ybor City Museum Society and Ybor City
Chamber of Commerce, Tampa
*Creative Arts Unlimited, Pinellas Park, Fla.*

The cigar industry has played a significant role in the development of Tampa, and Ybor City is an historic district of that city, home to some of its earliest Italian-American and Latin-American communities.

So the Ybor City Museum was an attempt by the Museum Society and local Chamber of Commerce to commemorate those histories. The design objective, says Roger Barganier, president of Creative Arts Unlimited (Pinellas Park, Fla.), was to create a 17,000-square-foot interior that would welcome, inform, exhibit artifacts and sell merchandise.

The retail area is fashioned after an 1890s cigar emporium and features framed antique cigar labels, photos, books, cigar ads and cigar paraphernalia. The perimeter case-work and fixturing echoes the style of turn-of-the-century woodwork common to the region.

Two stacked cigar boxes of Honduran mahogany and cedar form a cashwrap, from which oversized cigars float toward the ceiling. Each cigar belly-band contains the name of a sponsoring local business. The lid of the box, which serves as a partition wall defining the back of the theater area, incorporates the Chamber of Commerce logo in a vintage-style label.

In a carefully scaled re-creation of the district's first Spanish Community Theater, visitors can watch historic films about the area, seated in reproductions of rustic cigar rollers' chairs complete with nicotine-dyed leather coverings.

**CLIENT**
Ybor City Museum Society and Ybor City Chamber of Commerce, Tampa

**DESIGN**
Creative Arts Unlimited, Pinellas Park, Fla. – Roger Barganier, president

**DESIGN AND PROJECT MANAGEMENT**
Synergy Design Group, Tallahassee, Fla.

**OUTSIDE DESIGN CONSULTANTS**
Sweger Construction, Oldsmar, Fla. (general contractor); Lynn Rogers Design & Consulting, Tallahassee, Fla. (lighting); Steiner & Assoc., Tampa (developer)

**SUPPLIERS**
Creative Arts Unlimited, Pinellas Park, Fla. (fixtures, props, decoratives); Photobition, Atlanta (graphics)

**PHOTOGRAPHY**
Greg Wilson, Sarasota, Fla.

YBOR CITY
CHAMBER OF COMMERCE
VISITOR INFORMATION CENTER

# Four Seasons Coffee

Brookfield, Wis.

*KS Consulting, Milwaukee*

Four Seasons Coffee in Brookfield, Wis., was going to be surrounded by excellence, from the high-end office development it was moving into to the upscale residential neighborhoods that surround it. The clientele is discerning, and the products are all high quality (from the coffee to the bakery items to the sandwiches to the packaged foods and gift items).

This was no place for "just a cup of coffee," and KS Consulting (Milwaukee) was hired to help brand and design the new retail establishment with this in mind: the importance of differentiating the coffee shop from others in the area.

A branding workshop coordinated by KS Consulting established that the target market was "people who want to enjoy the entire coffee experience and are looking for great coffee," says Misha Corbin, KS's brand specialist.

"We decided to differentiate ourselves from the competition by offering an education station with tasting hours and coffee/tea information, along with the superior products and service," Corbin says. "And the objective was to empower our customers through knowledge, to create coffee connoisseurs who understood the value proposition."

KS left little to chance, using the focus group input to develop Four Seasons' name, logo, interior design, architecture, wall murals, menu design, graphic design elements, exterior signage – even staff dress code and training regimen. "All of these items are critical to reinforcing the brand message to the customer," says Corbin, "and creating an experience for them that results in a positive and lasting relationship."

The interior design and architecture reflect the brand through an uncluttered look and sense of "elegance and relaxation in an otherwise busy world." By incorporating curves and angles to create a sense of visual interest within the small (1563-square-foot) footprint, the flow of customer traffic can be more controlled and directed. Soffits bring the scale of the exposed ceiling to a more human level, as well, and define the zones of the process: ordering, pick-up and education. (The education stations provide information about the nuances and subtleties of any of Four Seasons' coffees.)

**CLIENT**
Four Seasons Coffee, Brookfield, Wis. – Connie and Mark Peppel, owners

**DESIGN**
KS Consulting, Milwaukee – Jeffrey Neidorfler, Misha Neidorfler, Kari Fetherston

**OUTSIDE DESIGN CONSULTANT**
Beyer Construction, New Berlin, Wis. (general contractor)

**PHOTOGRAPHY**
Kahler Slater, Brookfield, Wis.; Ed Purcell, Brookfield, Wis.

For more information on visual merchandising and store design, subscribe to:

Books on visual merchandising and store design available from ST Media Group International:

Budget Guide to Retail Store Planning & Design

In-Store Signage & Graphics: Connecting With Your Customer

Retail Store Planning & Design Manual, 2nd Ed.

Stores and Retail Spaces 1, 2, 3 & 4

Visual Merchandising 2 & 3

Visual Merchandising and Store Design Workbook

To subscribe, order books or to request a complete catalog of related books and magazines, please contact:

ST Media Group International Inc.

407 Gilbert Avenue

Cincinnati, Ohio 45202

Telephone: 1.800.925.1110 or 513.421.2050

Fax: 513.421.5144 or 513.421.6110

Email: books@stmediagroup.com

Web sites: visualstore (www.visualstore.com) and www.stmediagroup.com